# The Definition of Standard ML

# The Definition of Standard ML
# (Revised)

Robin Milner, Mads Tofte, Robert Harper and David MacQueen

The MIT Press
Cambridge, Massachusetts
London, England

Printed and bound in the United States of America.

Library of Congress Cataloging-in-Publication Data

The definition of standard ML: revised / Robin Milner ... et al.
    p.  cm.
  Includes bibliographical references and index.
  ISBN 0-262-63181-4 (alk. paper)
  1. ML (Computer program language)  I. Milner, R. (Robin), 1934-
QA76.73.M6D44  1997
005.13′3—dc21

                                            97-59
                                            CIP

# Contents

# Preface

A precise description of a programming language is a prerequisite for its implementation and for its use. The description can take many forms, each suited to a different purpose. A common form is a reference manual, which is usually a careful narrative description of the meaning of each construction in the language, often backed up with a formal presentation of the grammar (for example, in Backus-Naur form). This gives the programmer enough understanding for many of his purposes. But it is ill-suited for use by an implementer, or by someone who wants to formulate laws for equivalence of programs, or by a programmer who wants to design programs with mathematical rigour.

This document is a formal description of both the *grammar* and the *meaning* of a language which is both designed for large projects and widely used. As such, it aims to serve the whole community of people seriously concerned with the language. At a time when it is increasingly understood that programs must withstand rigorous analysis, particularly for systems where safety is critical, a rigorous language presentation is even important for negotiators and contractors; for a robust program written in an insecure language is like a house built upon sand.

Most people have not looked at a rigorous language presentation before. To help them particularly, but also to put the present work in perspective for those more theoretically prepared, it will be useful here to say something about three things: the nature of Standard ML, the task of language definition in general, and the form of the present Definition. We also briefly describe the recent revisions to the Definition.

## Standard ML

Standard ML is a functional programming language, in the sense that the full power of mathematical functions is present. But it grew in response to a particular programming task, for which it was equipped also with full imperative power, and a sophisticated exception mechanism. It has an advanced form of parametric modules, aimed at organised development of large programs. Finally it is strongly typed, and it was the first language to provide a particular form of polymorphic type which makes the strong typing remarkably flexible. This combination of ingredients has not made it unduly large, but their novelty has been a fascinating challenge to semantic method (of which we say more below).

ML has evolved over twenty years as a fusion of many ideas from many people. This evolution is described in some detail in Appendix F of the book, where also we acknowledge all those who have contributed to it, both in design and in implementation.

'ML' stands for *meta language*; this is the term logicians use for a language in which other (formal or informal) languages are discussed and analysed. Originally ML was conceived as a medium for finding and performing proofs in a logical language. Conducting rigorous argument as dialogue between person and machine has been a growing research topic throughout these twenty years. The difficulties are enormous, and make stern demands upon the programming language which is used for this dialogue. Those who are not familiar with computer-assisted reasoning may be surprised that a programming language, which was designed for this rather esoteric activity, should ever lay claim to being *generally* useful. On reflection, they should not be surprised. LISP is a prime example of a language invented for esoteric purposes and becoming widely used. LISP was invented for use in artificial intelligence (AI); the important thing about AI here is not that it is esoteric, but that it is difficult and varied; so much so, that anything which works well for it must work well for many other applications too.

The same can be said about the initial purpose of ML, but with a different emphasis. Rigorous proofs are complex things, which need varied and sophisticated presentation – particularly on the screen in interactive mode. Furthermore the proof methods, or strategies, involved are some of the most complex algorithms which we know. This all applies equally to AI, but one demand is made more strongly by proof than perhaps by any other application: the demand for rigour.

This demand established the character of ML. In order to be sure that, when the user and the computer claim to have together performed a rigorous argument, their claim is justified, it was seen that the language must be strongly typed. On the other hand, to be useful in a difficult application, the type system had to be rather flexible, and permit the machine to guide the user rather than impose a burden upon him. A reasonable solution was found, in which the machine helps the user significantly by inferring his types for him. Thereby the machine also confers complete reliability on his programs, in this sense: If a program claims that a certain result follows from the rules of reasoning which the user has supplied, then the claim may be fully trusted.

The principle of inferring useful structural information about programs is also represented, at the level of program modules, by the inference of *signatures*. Signatures describe the interfaces between modules, and are vital for robust large-scale programs. When the user combines modules, the signature discipline prevents him from mismatching their interfaces. By programming with interfaces and parametric modules, it becomes possible to focus on the structure of a large system, and to compile parts of it in isolation from one another – even when the system is incomplete.

This emphasis on types and signatures has had a profound effect on the language Definition. Over half this document is devoted to inferring types and signatures for programs. But the method used is exactly the same as for inferring what *values* a program delivers; indeed, a type or signature is the result of a kind of abstract evaluation of a program phrase.

In designing ML, the interplay among three activities – language design, definition and implementation – was extremely close. This was particularly true for the newest part, the parametric modules. This part of the language grew from an initial proposal by David MacQueen, itself highly developed; but both formal definition and implementation had a strong influence on the detailed design. In general, those who took part in the three activities cannot now imagine how they could have been properly done separately.

**Language Definition**

Every programming language presents its own conceptual view of computation. This view is usually indicated by the names used for the phrase classes of the language, or by its keywords: terms like package, module, structure, exception, channel, type, procedure, reference, sharing, .... These terms also have their abstract counterparts, which may be called *semantic objects*; these are what people really have in mind when they use the language, or discuss it, or think in it. Also, it is these objects, not the syntax, which represent the particular conceptual view of each language; they are the character of the language. Therefore a definition of the language must be in terms of these objects.

As is commonly done in programming language semantics, we shall loosely talk of these semantic objects as *meanings*. Of course, it is perfectly possible to understand the semantic theory of a language, and yet be unable to understand the meaning of a particular program, in the sense of its *intention* or *purpose*. The aim of a language definition is not to formalise everything which could possibly be called the meaning of a program, but to establish a theory of semantic objects upon which the understanding of particular programs may rest.

The job of a language-definer is twofold. First – as we have already suggested – he must create a world of meanings appropriate for the language, and must find a way of saying what these meanings precisely are. Here, he meets a problem; notation of *some* kind must be used to denote and describe these meanings – but not a *programming language* notation, unless he is passing the buck and defining one programming language in terms of another. Given a concern for rigour, mathematical notation is an obvious choice. Moreover, it is not enough just to write down mathematical definitions. The world of meanings only becomes meaningful if the objects possess nice properties, which make them tractable. So the language-definer really has to develop a small *theory* of his meanings, in the same way that a mathematician develops a theory. Typically, after initially defining some objects, the mathematician goes on to verify properties which indicate that they are objects worth studying. It is this part, a kind of scene-setting, which the language-definer shares with the mathematician. Of course he can take many objects and their theories directly from mathematics, such as functions, relations, trees, sequences, .... But he must also give some special theory for the objects which make his language particular, as we do for types, structures and signatures in this book; otherwise his language definition may be formal but will give no insight.

The second part of the definer's job is to define *evaluation* precisely. This means that he must define at least *what* meaning, $M$, results from evaluating any phrase $P$ of his language (though he need not explain exactly *how* the meaning results; that is he need not give the full detail of every computation). This part of his job must be formal to some extent, if only because the phrases $P$ of his language are indeed formal objects. But there is another reason for formality. The task is complex and error-prone, and therefore demands a high level of explicit organisation (which is, largely, the meaning of 'formality'); moreover, it will be used to specify an equally complex, error-prone and formal construction: an implementation.

We shall now explain the keystone of our semantic method. First, we need a slight but important refinement. A phrase $P$ is never evaluated *in vacuo* to a meaning $M$, but always *against a background*; this background – call it $B$ – is itself a semantic object, being a distillation of the meanings preserved from evaluation of earlier phrases (typically variable declarations, procedure declarations, etc.). In fact evaluation is background-dependent – $M$ depends upon $B$ as well as upon $P$.

The keystone of the method, then, is a certain kind of assertion about evaluation; it takes the form

$$B \vdash P \Rightarrow M$$

and may be pronounced: 'Against the background $B$, the phrase $P$ evaluates to the meaning $M$'. *The formal purpose of this Definition is no more, and no less, than to decree exactly which assertions of this form are true.* This could be achieved in many ways. We have chosen to do it in a structured way, as others have, by giving rules which allow assertions about a *compound* phrase $P$ to be inferred from assertions about its *constituent* phrases $P_1, \ldots, P_n$.

We have written the Definition in a form suggested by the previous remarks. That is, we have defined our semantic objects in mathematical notation which is completely independent of Standard ML, and we have developed just enough of their theory to give sense to our rules of evaluation.

Following another suggestion above, we have factored our task by describing *abstract* evaluation – the inference and checking of types and signatures (which can be done at compile-time) – completely separately from *concrete* evaluation. It really is a factorisation, because a *full* value in all its glory – you can think of it as a concrete object with a type attached – never has to be presented.

### The Revision of Standard ML

*The Definition of Standard ML* was published in 1990. Since then the implementation technology of the language has advanced enormously, and its users have multiplied. The language and its Definition have therefore incited close scrutiny, evaluation, much approval, sometimes strong criticism.

The originators of the language have sifted this response, and found that there are inadequacies in the original language and its formal Definition. They are of three kinds: missing features which many users want; complex and little-used features which most users can do without; and mistakes of definition. What is remarkable is that these inadequacies are rather few, and that they are rather uncontroversial.

This new version of the Definition addresses the three kinds of inadequacy respectively by additions, subtractions and corrections. But we have only made such amendments when one or more aspects of SML – the language itself, its usage, its implementation, its formal Definition – have thus become simpler, without complicating the other aspects. It is worth noting that even the additions meet this criterion; for example we have introduced type abbreviations in signatures to simplify the use of the language, but the way we have done it has even simplified the Definition too. In fact, after our changes the formal Definition has fewer rules.

In this exercise we have consulted the major implementers and several users, and have found broad agreement. In the 1990 Definition it was predicted that further versions of the Definition would be produced as the language develops, with the intention to minimise the number of versions. This is the first revised version, and we foresee no others. The changes that have been made to the 1990 Definition are enumerated in Appendix G.

The resulting document is, we hope, valuable as the essential point of reference for Standard ML. If it is to play this role well, it must be supplemented by other literature. Many expository books have already been written, and this Definition will be useful as a background reference for their readers. We became convinced, while writing the 1990 Definition, that we could not discuss many questions without making it far too long. Such questions are: Why were certain design choices made? What are their implications for programming? Was there a good alternative meaning for some constructs, or was our hand forced? What different forms of phrase are equivalent? What is the proof of certain claims? Many of these questions are not answered by pedagogic texts either. We therefore wrote a Commentary on the 1990 Definition to assist people in reading it, and to serve as a bridge between the Definition and other texts. Though in part outdated by the present revision, the Commentary still largely fulfils its purpose.

There exist several textbooks on programming with Standard ML[45,44,56,50]. The second edition of Paulson's book[45] conforms with the present revision.

We wish to thank Dave Berry, Lars Birkedal, Martin Elsman, Stefan Kahrs and John Reppy for many detailed comments and suggestions which have assisted the revision.

Robin Milner   Mads Tofte   Robert Harper   David MacQueen

November 1996

# 1 Introduction

This document formally defines Standard ML.

To understand the method of definition, at least in broad terms, it helps to consider how an implementation of ML is naturally organised. ML is an interactive language, and a *program* consists of a sequence of *top-level declarations*; the execution of each declaration modifies the top-level environment, which we call a *basis*, and reports the modification to the user.

In the execution of a declaration there are three phases: *parsing, elaboration,* and *evaluation.* Parsing determines the grammatical form of a declaration. Elaboration, the *static* phase, determines whether it is well-typed and well-formed in other ways, and records relevant type or form information in the basis. Finally evaluation, the *dynamic* phase, determines the value of the declaration and records relevant value information in the basis. Corresponding to these phases, our formal definition divides into three parts: grammatical rules, elaboration rules, and evaluation rules. Furthermore, the basis is divided into the *static* basis and the *dynamic* basis; for example, a variable which has been declared is associated with a type in the static basis and with a value in the dynamic basis.

In an implementation, the basis need not be so divided. But for the purpose of formal definition, it eases presentation and understanding to keep the static and dynamic parts of the basis separate. This is further justified by programming experience. A large proportion of errors in ML programs are discovered during elaboration, and identified as errors of type or form, so it follows that it is useful to perform the elaboration phase separately. In fact, elaboration without evaluation is part of what is normally called *compilation*; once a declaration (or larger entity) is compiled one wishes to evaluate it – repeatedly – without re-elaboration, from which it follows that it is useful to perform the evaluation phase separately.

A further factoring of the formal definition is possible, because of the structure of the language. ML consists of a lower level called the *Core language* (or *Core* for short), a middle level concerned with programming-in-the-large called *Modules*, and a very small upper level called *Programs*. With the three phases described above, there is therefore a possibility of nine components in the complete language definition. We have allotted one section to each of these components, except that we have combined the parsing, elaboration and evaluation of Programs in one section. The scheme for the ensuing seven sections is therefore as follows:

|                       | *Core*    | *Modules* | *Programs* |
|-----------------------|-----------|-----------|------------|
| *Syntax*              | Section 2 | Section 3 |            |
| *Static Semantics*    | Section 4 | Section 5 | Section 8  |
| *Dynamic Semantics*   | Section 6 | Section 7 |            |

The Core provides many phrase classes, for programming convenience. But about half of these classes are derived forms, whose meaning can be given by translation into the other half which we call the *Bare* language. Thus each of the three parts for the

Core treats only the bare language; the derived forms are treated in Appendix A. This appendix also contains a few derived forms for Modules. A full grammar for the language is presented in Appendix B.

In Appendices C and D the *initial basis* is detailed. This basis, divided into its static and dynamic parts, contains the static and dynamic meanings of a small set of predefined identifiers. A richer basis is defined in a separate document[18].

The semantics is presented in a form known as Natural Semantics. It consists of a set of rules allowing *sentences* of the form

$$A \vdash phrase \Rightarrow A'$$

to be inferred, where $A$ is often a basis (static or dynamic) and $A'$ a semantic object – often a type in the static semantics and a value in the dynamic semantics. One should read such a sentence as follows: "against the background provided by $A$, the phrase *phrase* elaborates – or evaluates – to the object $A'$". Although the rules themselves are formal the semantic objects, particularly the static ones, are the subject of a mathematical theory which is presented in a succinct form in the relevant sections.

The robustness of the semantics depends upon theorems. Usually these have been proven, but the proof is not included.

# 2 Syntax of the Core

## 2.1 Reserved Words

The following are the *reserved words* used in the Core. They may not (except `=` ) be used as identifiers.

```
abstype   and     andalso   as    case   datatype   do     else
end       exception   fn    fun   handle   if      in     infix
infixr    let     local    nonfix   of    op     open    orelse
raise     rec     then     type   val    with   withtype   while
( )       [ ]     { }    ,    :    ;    ...        _    |   =   =>   ->   #
```

## 2.2 Special constants

An *integer constant (in decimal notation)* is an optional negation symbol ($\tilde{\ }$) followed by a non-empty sequence of decimal digits $0, .., 9$. An *integer constant (in hexadecimal notation)* is an optional negation symbol followed by `0x` followed by a non-empty sequence of hexadecimal digits $0, .., 9$ and $a, .., f$. ($A, .., F$ may be used as alternatives for $a, .., f$.)

A *word constant (in decimal notation)* is `0w` followed by a non-empty sequence of decimal digits. A *word constant (in hexadecimal notation)* is `0wx` followed by a non-empty sequence of hexadecimal digits. A *real constant* is an integer constant in decimal notation, possibly followed by a point (`.`) and one or more decimal digits, possibly followed by an exponent symbol (`E` or `e`) and an integer constant in decimal notation; at least one of the optional parts must occur, hence no integer constant is a real constant. Examples: `0.7` `3.32E5` `3E~7` . Non-examples: `23` `.3` `4.E5` `1E2.0` .

We assume an underlying alphabet of $N$ characters ($N \geq 256$), numbered 0 to $N-1$, which agrees with the ASCII character set on the characters numbered 0 to 127. The interval $[0, N-1]$ is called the *ordinal range* of the alphabet. A *string constant* is a sequence, between quotes (`"`), of zero or more printable characters (i.e., numbered 33–126), spaces or escape sequences. Each escape sequence starts with the escape character `\` , and stands for a character sequence. The escape sequences are:

| | |
|---|---|
| `\a` | A single character interpreted by the system as alert (ASCII 7) |
| `\b` | Backspace (ASCII 8) |
| `\t` | Horizontal tab (ASCII 9) |
| `\n` | Linefeed, also known as newline (ASCII 10) |
| `\v` | Vertical tab (ASCII 11) |
| `\f` | Form feed (ASCII 12) |
| `\r` | Carriage return (ASCII 13) |
| `\^`$c$ | The control character $c$, where $c$ may be any character with number 64–95. The number of `\^`$c$ is 64 less than the number of $c$. |
| `\`$ddd$ | The single character with number $ddd$ (3 decimal digits denoting an integer in the ordinal range of the alphabet). |

\uxxxx   The single character with number $xxxx$ (4 hexadecimal digits denoting an integer in the ordinal range of the alphabet).

\"       "

\\       \

\$f \cdots f$\   This sequence is ignored, where $f \cdots f$ stands for a sequence of one
or more formatting characters.

The *formatting characters* are a subset of the non-printable characters including at
least space, tab, newline, formfeed. The last form allows long strings to be written on
more than one line, by writing \ at the end of one line and at the start of the next.

A *character constant* is a sequence of the form #$s$, where $s$ is a string constant denoting
a string of size one character.

Libraries may provide multiple numeric types and multiple string types. To each
string type corresponds an alphabet with ordinal range $[0, N - 1]$ for some $N \geq 256$;
each alphabet must agree with the ASCII character set on the characters numbered 0 to
127. When multiple alphabets are supported, all characters of a given string constant are
interpreted over the same alphabet. For each special constant, overloading resolution is
used for determining the type of the constant (see Appendix E).

We denote by SCon the class of *special constants*, i.e., the integer, real, word, character
and string constants; we shall use *scon* to range over SCon.

## 2.3 Comments

A *comment* is any character sequence within comment brackets (* *) in which comment
brackets are properly nested. No space is allowed between the two characters which make
up a comment bracket (* or *). An unmatched (* should be detected by the compiler.

## 2.4 Identifiers

The classes of *identifiers* for the Core are shown in Figure 1. We use *vid*, *tyvar* to
range over VId, TyVar etc. For each class X marked "long" there is a class longX of
*long identifiers*; if $x$ ranges over X then *longx* ranges over longX. The syntax of these long
identifiers is given by the following:

$$longx \quad ::= \quad x \qquad\qquad\qquad \text{identifier}$$
$$strid_1.\cdots.strid_n.x \quad \text{qualified identifier } (n \geq 1)$$

| VId | (value identifiers ) | long |
|-----|---------------------|------|
| TyVar | (type variables ) | |
| TyCon | (type constructors ) | long |
| Lab | (record labels ) | |
| StrId | (structure identifiers ) | long |

Figure 1: Identifiers

The qualified identifiers constitute a link between the Core and the Modules. Throughout this document, the term "identifier", occurring without an adjective, refers to non-qualified identifiers only.

An identifier is either *alphanumeric*: any sequence of letters, digits, primes (') and underbars (_) starting with a letter or prime, or *symbolic*: any non-empty sequence of the following *symbols*

$$! \quad \% \quad \& \quad \$ \quad \# \quad + \quad - \quad / \quad : \quad < \quad = \quad > \quad ? \quad @ \quad \backslash \quad \tilde{} \quad ` \quad \hat{} \quad | \quad *$$

In either case, however, reserved words are excluded. This means that for example # and | are not identifiers, but ## and |=| are identifiers. The only exception to this rule is that the symbol = , which is a reserved word, is also allowed as an identifier to stand for the equality predicate. The identifier = may not be re-bound; this precludes any syntactic ambiguity.

A type variable *tyvar* may be any alphanumeric identifier starting with a prime; the subclass EtyVar of TyVar, the *equality* type variables, consists of those which start with two or more primes. The classes VId, TyCon and Lab are represented by identifiers not starting with a prime. However, * is excluded from TyCon, to avoid confusion with the derived form of tuple type (see Figure 23). The class Lab is extended to include the *numeric* labels 1 2 3 ···, i.e. any numeral not starting with 0. The identifier class StrId is represented by alphanumeric identifiers not starting with a prime.

TyVar is therefore disjoint from the other four classes. Otherwise, the syntax class of an occurrence of identifier *id* in a Core phrase (ignoring derived forms, Section 2.7) is determined thus:

1. Immediately before "." – i.e. in a long identifier – or in an **open** declaration, *id* is a structure identifier. The following rules assume that all occurrences of structure identifiers have been removed.

2. At the start of a component in a record type, record pattern or record expression, *id* is a record label.

3. Elsewhere in types *id* is a type constructor.

4. Elsewhere, *id* is a value identifier.

By means of the above rules a compiler can determine the class to which each identifier occurrence belongs; for the remainder of this document we shall therefore assume that the classes are all disjoint.

## 2.5  Lexical analysis

Each item of lexical analysis is either a reserved word, a numeric label, a special constant or a long identifier. Comments and formatting characters separate items (except within string constants; see Section 2.2) and are otherwise ignored. At each stage the longest next item is taken.

## 2.6   Infixed operators

An identifier may be given *infix status* by the `infix` or `infixr` directive, which may occur as a declaration; this status only pertains to its use as a *vid* within the scope (see below) of the directive, and in these uses it is called an *infixed operator*. (Note that qualified identifiers never have infix status.) If *vid* has infix status, then "$exp_1\ vid\ exp_2$" (resp. "$pat_1\ vid\ pat_2$") may occur – in parentheses if necessary – wherever the application "$vid\{1=exp_1,2=exp_2\}$" or its derived form "$vid\,(exp_1,exp_2)$" (resp "$vid\,(pat_1,pat_2)$") would otherwise occur. On the other hand, an occurrence of any long identifier (qualified or not) prefixed by `op` is treated as non-infixed. The only required use of `op` is in prefixing a non-infixed occurrence of an identifier *vid* which has infix status; elsewhere `op`, where permitted, has no effect. Infix status is cancelled by the `nonfix` directive. We refer to the three directives collectively as *fixity directives*.

The form of the fixity directives is as follows ($n \geq 1$):

$$\texttt{infix}\ \langle d \rangle\ vid_1\ \cdots\ vid_n$$

$$\texttt{infixr}\ \langle d \rangle\ vid_1\ \cdots\ vid_n$$

$$\texttt{nonfix}\ vid_1\ \cdots\ vid_n$$

where $\langle d \rangle$ is an optional decimal digit $d$ indicating binding precedence. A higher value of $d$ indicates tighter binding; the default is 0. `infix` and `infixr` dictate left and right associativity respectively. In an expression of the form $exp_1\ vid_1\ exp_2\ vid_2\ exp_3$, where $vid_1$ and $vid_2$ are infixed operators with the same precedence, either both must associate to the left or both must associate to the right. For example, suppose that `<<` and `>>` have equal precedence, but associate to the left and right respectively; then

| | | |
|---|---|---|
| `x << y << z` | parses as | `(x << y) << z` |
| `x >> y >> z` | parses as | `x >> (y >> z)` |
| `x << y >> z` | is illegal | |
| `x >> y << z` | is illegal | |

The precedence of infixed operators relative to other expression and pattern constructions is given in Appendix B.

The *scope* of a fixity directive *dir* is the ensuing program text, except that if *dir* occurs in a declaration *dec* in either of the phrases

$$\texttt{let}\ dec\ \texttt{in}\ \cdots\ \texttt{end}$$

$$\texttt{local}\ dec\ \texttt{in}\ \cdots\ \texttt{end}$$

then the scope of *dir* does not extend beyond the phrase. Further scope limitations are imposed for Modules (see Section 3.3).

These directives and `op` are omitted from the semantic rules, since they affect only parsing.

| AtExp | atomic expressions |
| ExpRow | expression rows |
| Exp | expressions |
| Match | matches |
| Mrule | match rules |
| Dec | declarations |
| ValBind | value bindings |
| TypBind | type bindings |
| DatBind | datatype bindings |
| ConBind | constructor bindings |
| ExBind | exception bindings |
| AtPat | atomic patterns |
| PatRow | pattern rows |
| Pat | patterns |
| Ty | type expressions |
| TyRow | type-expression rows |

Figure 2: Core Phrase Classes

## 2.7   Derived Forms

There are many standard syntactic forms in ML whose meaning can be expressed in terms of a smaller number of syntactic forms, called the *bare* language. These derived forms, and their equivalent forms in the bare language, are given in Appendix A.

## 2.8   Grammar

The phrase classes for the Core are shown in Figure 2. We use the variable *atexp* to range over AtExp, etc. The grammatical rules for the Core are shown in Figures 3 and 4.

The following conventions are adopted in presenting the grammatical rules, and in their interpretation:

- The brackets ⟨ ⟩ enclose optional phrases.

- For any syntax class X (over which *x* ranges) we define the syntax class Xseq (over which *xseq* ranges) as follows:

$$xseq \quad ::= \quad x \qquad \qquad \text{(singleton sequence)}$$
$$\text{(empty sequence)}$$
$$(x_1, \cdots, x_n) \quad \text{(sequence, } n \geq 1)$$

(Note that the "···" used here, meaning syntactic iteration, must not be confused with "..." which is a reserved word of the language.)

- Alternative forms for each phrase class are in order of decreasing precedence; this resolves ambiguity in parsing, as explained in Appendix B.

- L (resp. R) means left (resp. right) association.

- The syntax of types binds more tightly than that of expressions.

- Each iterated construct (e.g. *match*, ⋯) extends as far right as possible; thus, parentheses may be needed around an expression which terminates with a match, e.g. "fn *match*", if this occurs within a larger match.

| | | | |
|---|---|---|---|
| *atpat* | ::= | _ | wildcard |
| | | *scon* | special constant |
| | | ⟨op⟩*longvid* | value identifier |
| | | { ⟨*patrow*⟩ } | record |
| | | ( *pat* ) | |
| *patrow* | ::= | ... | wildcard |
| | | *lab* = *pat* ⟨ , *patrow*⟩ | pattern row |
| *pat* | ::= | *atpat* | atomic |
| | | ⟨op⟩*longvid atpat* | constructed pattern |
| | | *pat*₁ *vid* *pat*₂ | infixed value construction |
| | | *pat* : *ty* | typed |
| | | ⟨op⟩*vid*⟨: *ty*⟩ as *pat* | layered |
| *ty* | ::= | *tyvar* | type variable |
| | | { ⟨*tyrow*⟩ } | record type expression |
| | | *tyseq longtycon* | type construction |
| | | *ty* -> *ty*′ | function type expression (R) |
| | | ( *ty* ) | |
| *tyrow* | ::= | *lab* : *ty* ⟨ , *tyrow*⟩ | type-expression row |

Figure 3: Grammar: Patterns and Type expressions

## 2.9   Syntactic Restrictions

- No expression row, pattern row or type-expression row may bind the same *lab* twice.

- No binding *valbind*, *typbind*, *datbind* or *exbind* may bind the same identifier twice; this applies also to value identifiers within a *datbind*.

- No *tyvarseq* may contain the same *tyvar* twice.

- For each value binding *pat* = *exp* within rec, *exp* must be of the form fn *match*. The derived form of function-value binding given in Appendix A, page 57, necessarily obeys this restriction.

- No *datbind*, *valbind* or *exbind* may bind `true`, `false`, `nil`, `::` or `ref`. No *datbind* or *exbind* may bind `it`.

- No real constant may occur in a pattern.

- In a value declaration `val` *tyvarseq valbind*, if *valbind* contains another value declaration `val` *tyvarseq' valbind'* then *tyvarseq* and *tyvarseq'* must be disjoint. In other words, no type variable may be scoped by two value declarations of which one occurs inside the other. This restriction applies after *tyvarseq* and *tyvarseq'* have been extended to include implicitly scoped type variables, as explained in Section 4.6.

| *atexp* | ::= | *scon* | special constant |
| | | ⟨op⟩*longvid* | value identifier |
| | | { ⟨*exprow*⟩ } | record |
| | | let *dec* in *exp* end | local declaration |
| | | ( *exp* ) | |
| *exprow* | ::= | *lab* = *exp* ⟨ , *exprow*⟩ | expression row |
| *exp* | ::= | *atexp* | atomic |
| | | *exp* *atexp* | application (L) |
| | | $exp_1$ *vid* $exp_2$ | infixed application |
| | | *exp* : *ty* | typed (L) |
| | | *exp* handle *match* | handle exception |
| | | raise *exp* | raise exception |
| | | fn *match* | function |
| *match* | ::= | *mrule* ⟨ \| *match*⟩ | |
| *mrule* | ::= | *pat* => *exp* | |
| *dec* | ::= | val *tyvarseq* *valbind* | value declaration |
| | | type *typbind* | type declaration |
| | | datatype *datbind* | datatype declaration |
| | | datatype *tycon* = datatype *longtycon* | datatype replication |
| | | abstype *datbind* with *dec* end | abstype declaration |
| | | exception *exbind* | exception declaration |
| | | local $dec_1$ in $dec_2$ end | local declaration |
| | | open $longstrid_1$ ⋯ $longstrid_n$ | open declaration ($n \geq 1$) |
| | | | empty declaration |
| | | $dec_1$ ⟨;⟩ $dec_2$ | sequential declaration |
| | | infix ⟨*d*⟩ $vid_1$ ⋯ $vid_n$ | infix (L) directive |
| | | infixr ⟨*d*⟩ $vid_1$ ⋯ $vid_n$ | infix (R) directive |
| | | nonfix $vid_1$ ⋯ $vid_n$ | nonfix directive |
| *valbind* | ::= | *pat* = *exp* ⟨and *valbind*⟩ | |
| | | rec *valbind* | |
| *typbind* | ::= | *tyvarseq* *tycon* = *ty* ⟨and *typbind*⟩ | |
| *datbind* | ::= | *tyvarseq* *tycon* = *conbind* ⟨and *datbind*⟩ | |
| *conbind* | ::= | ⟨op⟩*vid* ⟨of *ty*⟩ ⟨ \| *conbind*⟩ | |
| *exbind* | ::= | ⟨op⟩*vid* ⟨of *ty*⟩ ⟨and *exbind*⟩ | |
| | | ⟨op⟩*vid* = ⟨op⟩*longvid* ⟨and *exbind*⟩ | |

Figure 4: Grammar: Expressions, Matches, Declarations and Bindings

# 3   Syntax of Modules

For Modules there are further reserved words, identifier classes and derived forms. There are no further special constants; comments and lexical analysis are as for the Core. The derived forms for modules appear in Appendix A.

## 3.1   Reserved Words

The following are the additional reserved words used in Modules.

```
eqtype    functor   include   sharing   sig
signature  struct   structure  where    :>
```

## 3.2   Identifiers

The additional identifier classes for Modules are SigId (signature identifiers) and FunId (functor identifiers). Functor and signature identifiers must be alphanumeric, not starting with a prime. The class of each identifier occurrence is determined by the grammatical rules which follow. Henceforth, therefore, we consider all identifier classes to be disjoint.

## 3.3   Infixed operators

In addition to the scope rules for fixity directives given for the Core syntax, there is a further scope limitation: if *dir* occurs in a structure-level declaration *strdec* in any of the phrases

$$\texttt{let } strdec \texttt{ in } \cdots \texttt{ end}$$

$$\texttt{local } strdec \texttt{ in } \cdots \texttt{ end}$$

$$\texttt{struct } strdec \texttt{ end}$$

then the scope of *dir* does not extend beyond the phrase.

One effect of this limitation is that fixity is local to a basic structure expression — in particular, to such an expression occurring as a functor body.

## 3.4   Grammar for Modules

The phrase classes for Modules are shown in Figure 5. We use the variable *strexp* to range over StrExp, etc. The conventions adopted in presenting the grammatical rules for Modules are the same as for the Core. The grammatical rules are shown in Figures 6, 7 and 8.

| StrExp | structure expressions |
| StrDec | structure-level declarations |
| StrBind | structure bindings |
| | |
| SigExp | signature expressions |
| SigDec | signature declarations |
| SigBind | signature bindings |
| | |
| Spec | specifications |
| ValDesc | value descriptions |
| TypDesc | type descriptions |
| DatDesc | datatype descriptions |
| ConDesc | constructor descriptions |
| ExDesc | exception descriptions |
| StrDesc | structure descriptions |
| | |
| FunDec | functor declarations |
| FunBind | functor bindings |
| TopDec | top-level declarations |

Figure 5: Modules Phrase Classes

## 3.5   Syntactic Restrictions

- No binding *strbind*, *sigbind*, or *funbind* may bind the same identifier twice.

- No description *valdesc*, *typdesc*, *datdesc*, *exdesc* or *strdesc* may describe the same identifier twice; this applies also to value identifiers within a *datdesc*.

- No *tyvarseq* may contain the same *tyvar* twice.

- Any *tyvar* occurring on the right side of a *datdesc* of the form *tyvarseq tycon* = $\cdots$ must occur in the *tyvarseq*; similarly, in signature expressions of the form *sigexp* where type *tyvarseq longtycon* = *ty*, any *tyvar* occurring in *ty* must occur in *tyvarseq*.

- No *datdesc*, *valdesc* or *exdesc* may describe true, false, nil, :: or ref. No *datdesc* or *exdesc* may describe it.

| *strexp* | ::= | **struct** *strdec* **end** | basic |
| | | *longstrid* | structure identifier |
| | | *strexp* : *sigexp* | transparent constraint |
| | | *strexp* :>*sigexp* | opaque constraint |
| | | *funid* ( *strexp* ) | functor application |
| | | **let** *strdec* **in** *strexp* **end** | local declaration |
| *strdec* | ::= | *dec* | declaration |
| | | **structure** *strbind* | structure |
| | | **local** *strdec₁* **in** *strdec₂* **end** | local |
| | | | empty |
| | | *strdec₁* ⟨;⟩ *strdec₂* | sequential |
| *strbind* | ::= | *strid* = *strexp* ⟨**and** *strbind*⟩ | |
| *sigexp* | ::= | **sig** *spec* **end** | basic |
| | | *sigid* | signature identifier |
| | | *sigexp* **where type** | type realisation |
| | |     *tyvarseq longtycon* = *ty* | |
| *sigdec* | ::= | **signature** *sigbind* | |
| *sigbind* | ::= | *sigid* = *sigexp* ⟨**and** *sigbind*⟩ | |

Figure 6: Grammar: Structure and Signature Expressions

| *spec* | ::= | **val** *valdesc* | value |
|---|---|---|---|
| | | **type** *typdesc* | type |
| | | **eqtype** *typdesc* | eqtype |
| | | **datatype** *datdesc* | datatype |
| | | **datatype** *tycon* = **datatype** *longtycon* | replication |
| | | **exception** *exdesc* | exception |
| | | **structure** *strdesc* | structure |
| | | **include** *sigexp* | include |
| | | | empty |
| | | *spec*$_1$ ⟨;⟩ *spec*$_2$ | sequential |
| | | *spec* **sharing type** | sharing |
| | | *longtycon*$_1$ = ⋯ = *longtycon*$_n$ | $(n \geq 2)$ |

| *valdesc* | ::= | *vid* : *ty* ⟨**and** *valdesc*⟩ |
|---|---|---|
| *typdesc* | ::= | *tyvarseq tycon* ⟨**and** *typdesc*⟩ |
| *datdesc* | ::= | *tyvarseq tycon* = *condesc* ⟨**and** *datdesc*⟩ |
| *condesc* | ::= | *vid* ⟨**of** *ty*⟩ ⟨ | *condesc*⟩ |
| *exdesc* | ::= | *vid* ⟨**of** *ty*⟩ ⟨**and** *exdesc*⟩ |
| *strdesc* | ::= | *strid* : *sigexp* ⟨**and** *strdesc*⟩ |

Figure 7: Grammar: Specifications

| *fundec* | ::= | **functor** *funbind* | |
|---|---|---|---|
| *funbind* | ::= | *funid* ( *strid* : *sigexp* ) = *strexp* | functor binding |
| | | ⟨**and** *funbind*⟩ | |
| *topdec* | ::= | *strdec* ⟨*topdec*⟩ | structure-level declaration |
| | | *sigdec* ⟨*topdec*⟩ | signature declaration |
| | | *fundec* ⟨*topdec*⟩ | functor declaration |

*Restriction:* No *topdec* may contain, as an initial segment, a *strdec* followed by a semicolon.

Figure 8: Grammar: Functors and Top-level Declarations

# 4   Static Semantics for the Core

Our first task in presenting the semantics – whether for Core or Modules, static or dynamic – is to define the objects concerned. In addition to the class of *syntactic* objects, which we have already defined, there are classes of so-called *semantic* objects used to describe the meaning of the syntactic objects. Some classes contain *simple* semantic objects; such objects are usually identifiers or names of some kind. Other classes contain *compound* semantic objects, such as types or environments, which are constructed from component objects.

## 4.1   Simple Objects

All semantic objects in the static semantics of the entire language are built from identifiers and two further kinds of simple objects: type constructor names and identifier status descriptors. Type constructor names are the values taken by type constructors; we shall usually refer to them briefly as type names, but they are to be clearly distinguished from type variables and type constructors. The simple object classes, and the variables ranging over them, are shown in Figure 9. We have included TyVar in the table to make visible the use of $\alpha$ in the semantics to range over TyVar.

$$
\begin{array}{rcll}
\alpha \text{ or } tyvar & \in & \text{TyVar} & \text{type variables} \\
t & \in & \text{TyName} & \text{type names} \\
is & \in & \text{IdStatus} = \{\mathsf{c}, \mathsf{e}, \mathsf{v}\} & \text{identifier status descriptors}
\end{array}
$$

Figure 9: Simple Semantic Objects

Each $\alpha \in$ TyVar possesses a boolean *equality* attribute, which determines whether or not it *admits equality*, i.e. whether it is a member of EtyVar (defined on page 5).

Each $t \in$ TyName has an arity $k \geq 0$, and also possesses an equality attribute. We denote the class of type names with arity $k$ by TyName$^{(k)}$.

With each special constant *scon* we associate a type name type(*scon*) which is either `int`, `real`, `word`, `char` or `string` as indicated by Section 2.2. (However, see Appendix E concerning types of overloaded special constants.)

## 4.2   Compound Objects

When $A$ and $B$ are sets Fin $A$ denotes the set of finite subsets of $A$, and $A \xrightarrow{\text{fin}} B$ denotes the set of *finite maps* (partial functions with finite domain) from $A$ to $B$. The domain and range of a finite map, $f$, are denoted Dom $f$ and Ran $f$. A finite map will often be written explicitly in the form $\{a_1 \mapsto b_1, \cdots, a_k \mapsto b_k\}$, $k \geq 0$; in particular the empty map is $\{\}$. We shall use the form $\{x \mapsto e \; ; \; \phi\}$ – a form of set comprehension – to stand for the finite map $f$ whose domain is the set of values $x$ which satisfy the condition $\phi$, and whose value on this domain is given by $f(x) = e$.

When $f$ and $g$ are finite maps the map $f + g$, called $f$ *modified* by $g$, is the finite map with domain $\mathrm{Dom}\, f \cup \mathrm{Dom}\, g$ and values

$$(f + g)(a) = \text{if } a \in \mathrm{Dom}\, g \text{ then } g(a) \text{ else } f(a).$$

The compound objects for the static semantics of the Core Language are shown in Figure 10. We take $\cup$ to mean disjoint union over semantic object classes. We also understand all the defined object classes to be disjoint.

$$
\begin{aligned}
\tau &\in \text{Type} = \text{TyVar} \cup \text{RowType} \cup \text{FunType} \cup \text{ConsType} \\
(\tau_1, \cdots, \tau_k) \text{ or } \tau^{(k)} &\in \text{Type}^k \\
(\alpha_1, \cdots, \alpha_k) \text{ or } \alpha^{(k)} &\in \text{TyVar}^k \\
\varrho &\in \text{RowType} = \text{Lab} \overset{\text{fin}}{\to} \text{Type} \\
\tau \to \tau' &\in \text{FunType} = \text{Type} \times \text{Type} \\
&\quad \text{ConsType} = \cup_{k \geq 0} \text{ConsType}^{(k)} \\
\tau^{(k)} t &\in \text{ConsType}^{(k)} = \text{Type}^k \times \text{TyName}^{(k)} \\
\theta \text{ or } \Lambda \alpha^{(k)}.\tau &\in \text{TypeFcn} = \cup_{k \geq 0} \text{TyVar}^k \times \text{Type} \\
\sigma \text{ or } \forall \alpha^{(k)}.\tau &\in \text{TypeScheme} = \cup_{k \geq 0} \text{TyVar}^k \times \text{Type} \\
(\theta, VE) &\in \text{TyStr} = \text{TypeFcn} \times \text{ValEnv} \\
SE &\in \text{StrEnv} = \text{StrId} \overset{\text{fin}}{\to} \text{Env} \\
TE &\in \text{TyEnv} = \text{TyCon} \overset{\text{fin}}{\to} \text{TyStr} \\
VE &\in \text{ValEnv} = \text{VId} \overset{\text{fin}}{\to} \text{TypeScheme} \times \text{IdStatus} \\
E \text{ or } (SE, TE, VE) &\in \text{Env} = \text{StrEnv} \times \text{TyEnv} \times \text{ValEnv} \\
T &\in \text{TyNameSet} = \text{Fin}(\text{TyName}) \\
U &\in \text{TyVarSet} = \text{Fin}(\text{TyVar}) \\
C \text{ or } T, U, E &\in \text{Context} = \text{TyNameSet} \times \text{TyVarSet} \times \text{Env}
\end{aligned}
$$

Figure 10: Compound Semantic Objects

Note that $\Lambda$ and $\forall$ bind type variables. For any semantic object $A$, tynames $A$ and tyvars $A$ denote respectively the set of type names and the set of type variables occurring free in $A$.

Also note that a value environment maps value identifiers to a pair of a type scheme and an identifier status. If $VE(vid) = (\sigma, is)$, we say that *vid has status is in VE*. An occurrence of a value identifier which is elaborated in $VE$ is referred to as a *value variable*, a *value constructor* or an *exception constructor*, depending on whether its status in $VE$ is v, c or e, respectively.

## 4.3   Projection, Injection and Modification

**Projection**: We often need to select components of tuples – for example, the value-environment component of a context. In such cases we rely on metavariable names to indicate which component is selected. For instance "*VE* of *E*" means "the value-environment component of *E*".

Moreover, when a tuple contains a finite map we shall "apply" the tuple to an argument, relying on the syntactic class of the argument to determine the relevant function. For instance $C(tycon)$ means $(TE \text{ of } C)tycon$ and $C(vid)$ means $(VE \text{ of } (E \text{ of } C))(vid)$.

Finally, environments may be applied to long identifiers. For instance if $longvid = strid_1.\cdots.strid_k.vid$ then $E(longvid)$ means

$$(VE \text{ of } (SE \text{ of } \cdots(SE \text{ of } (SE \text{ of } E)strid_1)strid_2\cdots)strid_k)vid.$$

**Injection**:   Components may be injected into tuple classes; for example, "*VE* in Env" means the environment $(\{\}, \{\}, VE)$.

**Modification**: The modification of one map $f$ by another map $g$, written $f + g$, has already been mentioned. It is commonly used for environment modification, for example $E + E'$. Often, empty components will be left implicit in a modification; for example $E + VE$ means $E + (\{\}, \{\}, VE)$. For set components, modification means union, so that $C + (T, VE)$ means

$$(\ (T \text{ of } C) \cup T,\ U \text{ of } C,\ (E \text{ of } C) + VE\ )$$

Finally, we frequently need to modify a context $C$ by an environment $E$ (or a type environment $TE$ say), at the same time extending $T$ of $C$ to include the type names of $E$ (or of $TE$ say). We therefore define $C \oplus TE$, for example, to mean $C + (\text{tynames } TE, TE)$.

## 4.4   Types and Type functions

A type $\tau$ is an *equality type*, or *admits equality*, if it is of one of the forms

- $\alpha$, where $\alpha$ admits equality;

- $\{lab_1 \mapsto \tau_1,\ \cdots,\ lab_n \mapsto \tau_n\}$, where each $\tau_i$ admits equality;

- $\tau^{(k)}t$, where $t$ and all members of $\tau^{(k)}$ admit equality;

- $(\tau')\mathbf{ref}$.

A type function $\theta = \Lambda\alpha^{(k)}.\tau$ has arity $k$; the bound variables must be distinct. Two type functions are considered equal if they only differ in their choice of bound variables (alpha-conversion). In particular, the equality attribute has no significance in a bound variable of a type function; for example, $\Lambda\alpha.\alpha \to \alpha$ and $\Lambda\beta.\beta \to \beta$ are equal type functions even if $\alpha$ admits equality but $\beta$ does not. If $t$ has arity $k$, then we write $t$ to mean $\Lambda\alpha^{(k)}.\alpha^{(k)}t$ (eta-conversion); thus TyName $\subseteq$ TypeFcn. $\theta = \Lambda\alpha^{(k)}.\tau$ is an *equality* type function, or *admits equality*, if when the type variables $\alpha^{(k)}$ are chosen to admit equality then $\tau$ also admits equality.

We write the application of a type function $\theta$ to a vector $\tau^{(k)}$ of types as $\tau^{(k)}\theta$. If $\theta = \Lambda\alpha^{(k)}.\tau$ we set $\tau^{(k)}\theta = \tau\{\tau^{(k)}/\alpha^{(k)}\}$ (beta-conversion).

We write $\tau\{\theta^{(k)}/t^{(k)}\}$ for the result of substituting type functions $\theta^{(k)}$ for type names $t^{(k)}$ in $\tau$. We assume that all beta-conversions are carried out after substitution, so that for example

$$(\tau^{(k)}t)\{\Lambda\alpha^{(k)}.\tau/t\} = \tau\{\tau^{(k)}/\alpha^{(k)}\}.$$

## 4.5   Type Schemes

A type scheme $\sigma = \forall\alpha^{(k)}.\tau$ *generalises* a type $\tau'$, written $\sigma \succ \tau'$, if $\tau' = \tau\{\tau^{(k)}/\alpha^{(k)}\}$ for some $\tau^{(k)}$, where each member $\tau_i$ of $\tau^{(k)}$ admits equality if $\alpha_i$ does. If $\sigma' = \forall\beta^{(l)}.\tau'$ then $\sigma$ *generalises* $\sigma'$, written $\sigma \succ \sigma'$, if $\sigma \succ \tau'$ and $\beta^{(l)}$ contains no free type variable of $\sigma$. It can be shown that $\sigma \succ \sigma'$ iff, for all $\tau''$, whenever $\sigma' \succ \tau''$ then also $\sigma \succ \tau''$.

Two type schemes $\sigma$ and $\sigma'$ are considered equal if they can be obtained from each other by renaming and reordering of bound type variables, and deleting type variables from the prefix which do not occur in the body. Here, in contrast to the case for type functions, the equality attribute must be preserved in renaming; for example $\forall\alpha.\alpha \to \alpha$ and $\forall\beta.\beta \to \beta$ are only equal if either both $\alpha$ and $\beta$ admit equality, or neither does. It can be shown that $\sigma = \sigma'$ iff $\sigma \succ \sigma'$ and $\sigma' \succ \sigma$.

We consider a type $\tau$ to be a type scheme, identifying it with $\forall().\tau$.

## 4.6   Scope of Explicit Type Variables

In the Core language, a type or datatype binding can explicitly introduce type variables whose scope is that binding. Moreover, in a value declaration **val** *tyvarseq valbind*, the sequence *tyvarseq* binds type variables: a type variable occurs free in **val** *tyvarseq valbind* iff it occurs free in *valbind* and is not in the sequence *tyvarseq*. However, explicit binding of type variables at **val** is optional, so we still have to account for the scope of an explicit type variable occurring in the ": *ty*" of a typed expression or pattern or in the "**of** *ty*" of an exception binding. For the rest of this section, we consider such free occurrences of type variables only.

Every occurrence of a value declaration is said to *scope* a set of explicit type variables determined as follows.

First, a free occurrence of $\alpha$ in a value declaration **val** *tyvarseq valbind* is said to be *unguarded* if the occurrence is not part of a smaller value declaration within *valbind*. In this case we say that $\alpha$ *occurs unguarded* in the value declaration.

Then we say that $\alpha$ is *implicitly scoped* at a particular value declaration **val** *tyvarseq valbind* in a program if (1) $\alpha$ occurs unguarded in this value declaration, and (2) $\alpha$ does not occur unguarded in any larger value declaration containing the given one.

Henceforth, we assume that for every value declaration val *tyvarseq*··· occurring in the program, every explicit type variable implicitly scoped at the val has been added to *tyvarseq* (subject to the syntactic constraint in Section 2.9). Thus for example, in the two declarations

```
val x = let val id:'a->'a = fn z=>z in id id end
val x = (let val id:'a->'a = fn z=>z in id id end; fn z=>z:'a)
```

the type variable 'a is scoped differently; they become respectively

```
val x = let val 'a id:'a->'a = fn z=>z in id id end
val 'a x = (let val id:'a->'a = fn z=>z in id id end; fn z=>z:'a)
```

Then, according to the inference rules in Section 4.10 the first example can be elaborated, but the second cannot since 'a is bound at the outer value declaration leaving no possibility of two different instantiations of the type of id in the application id id.

## 4.7   Non-expansive Expressions

In order to treat polymorphic references and exceptions, the set Exp of expressions is partitioned into two classes, the *expansive* and the *non-expansive* expressions. An expression is *non-expansive in context* $C$ if, after replacing infixed forms by their equivalent prefixed forms, and derived forms by their equivalent forms, it can be generated by the following grammar from the non-terminal *nexp*:

| | | | | | |
|---|---|---|---|---|---|
| *nexp* | ::= | *scon* | *nexprow* | ::= | *lab* = *nexp*⟨, *nexprow*⟩ |
| | | ⟨op⟩*longvid* | | | |
| | | {⟨*nexprow*⟩} | *conexp* | ::= | (*conexp*⟨:*ty*⟩) |
| | | (*nexp*) | | | ⟨op⟩*longvid* |
| | | *conexp* *nexp* | | | |
| | | *nexp*:*ty* | | | |
| | | fn *match* | | | |

*Restriction:* Within a *conexp*, we require *longvid* ≠ ref and *is* of $C(longvid) \in \{c, e\}$.

All other expressions are said to be *expansive (in C)*. The idea is that the dynamic evaluation of a non-expansive expression will neither generate an exception nor extend the domain of the memory, while the evaluation of an expansive expression might.

## 4.8   Closure

Let $\tau$ be a type and $A$ a semantic object. Then $\text{Clos}_A(\tau)$, the *closure* of $\tau$ with respect to $A$, is the type scheme $\forall \alpha^{(k)}.\tau$, where $\alpha^{(k)} = \text{tyvars}(\tau) \setminus \text{tyvars} A$. Commonly, $A$ will be a context $C$. We abbreviate the *total* closure $\text{Clos}_{\{\}}(\tau)$ to $\text{Clos}(\tau)$. If the range of a value environment *VE* contains only types (rather than arbitrary type schemes) we set

$$\text{Clos}_A VE = \{vid \mapsto (\text{Clos}_A(\tau), is) \; ; \; VE(vid) = (\tau, is)\}$$

Closing a value environment $VE$ that stems from the elaboration of a value binding *valbind* requires extra care to ensure type security of references and exceptions and correct scoping of explicit type variables. Recall that *valbind* is not allowed to bind the same variable twice. Thus, for each $vid \in \text{Dom}\, VE$ there is a unique *pat* = *exp* in *valbind* which binds *vid*. If $VE(vid) = (\tau, is)$, let $\text{Clos}_{C,valbind} VE(vid) = (\forall \alpha^{(k)}.\tau, is)$, where

$$\alpha^{(k)} = \begin{cases} \text{tyvars}\, \tau \setminus \text{tyvars}\, C, & \text{if } exp \text{ is non-expansive in } C; \\ (), & \text{if } exp \text{ is expansive in } C. \end{cases}$$

## 4.9   Type Structures and Type Environments

A type structure $(\theta, VE)$ is *well-formed* if either $VE = \{\}$, or $\theta$ is a type name $t$. (The latter case arises, with $VE \neq \{\}$, in **datatype** declarations.) An object or assembly $A$ of semantic objects is *well-formed* if every type structure occurring in $A$ is well-formed.

A type structure $(t, VE)$ is said to *respect equality* if, whenever $t$ admits equality, then either $t = \mathbf{ref}$ (see Appendix C) or, for each $VE(vid)$ of the form $(\forall \alpha^{(k)}.(\tau \rightarrow \alpha^{(k)}t), is)$, the type function $\Lambda \alpha^{(k)}.\tau$ also admits equality. (This ensures that the equality predicate = will be applicable to a constructed value $(vid, v)$ of type $\tau^{(k)}t$ only when it is applicable to the value $v$ itself, whose type is $\tau\{\tau^{(k)}/\alpha^{(k)}\}$.) A type environment $TE$ *respects equality* if all its type structures do so.

Let $TE$ be a type environment, and let $T$ be the set of type names $t$ such that $(t, VE)$ occurs in $TE$ for some $VE \neq \{\}$. Then $TE$ is said to *maximise equality* if (a) $TE$ respects equality, and also (b) if any larger subset of $T$ were to admit equality (without any change in the equality attribute of any type names not in $T$) then $TE$ would cease to respect equality.

For any $TE$ of the form

$$TE = \{tycon_i \mapsto (t_i, VE_i) \; ; \; 1 \leq i \leq k\},$$

where no $VE_i$ is the empty map, and for any $E$ we define $\text{Abs}(TE, E)$ to be the environment obtained from $E$ and $TE$ as follows. First, let $\text{Abs}(TE)$ be the type environment $\{tycon_i \mapsto (t_i, \{\}) \; ; \; 1 \leq i \leq k\}$ in which all value environments $VE_i$ have been replaced by the empty map. Let $t'_1, \cdots, t'_k$ be new distinct type names none of which admit equality. Then $\text{Abs}(TE, E)$ is the result of simultaneously substituting $t'_i$ for $t_i$, $1 \leq i \leq k$, throughout $\text{Abs}(TE) + E$. (The effect of the latter substitution is to ensure that the use of equality on an **abstype** is restricted to the **with** part.)

## 4.10   Inference Rules

Each rule of the semantics allows inferences among sentences of the form

$$A \vdash phrase \Rightarrow A'$$

where $A$ is usually a context, *phrase* is a phrase of the Core, and $A'$ is a semantic object – usually a type or an environment. It may be pronounced "*phrase* elaborates to $A'$ in (context) $A$". Some rules have extra hypotheses not of this form; they are called *side conditions*.

In the presentation of the rules, phrases within single angle brackets $\langle \; \rangle$ are called *first options*, and those within double angle brackets $\langle\langle \; \rangle\rangle$ are called *second options*. To reduce the number of rules, we have adopted the following convention:

> In each instance of a rule, the first options must be either all present or all absent; similarly the second options must be either all present or all absent.

Although not assumed in our definitions, it is intended that every context $C = T, U, E$ has the property that tynames $E \subseteq T$. Thus $T$ may be thought of, loosely, as containing all type names which "have been generated". It is necessary to include $T$ as a separate component in a context, since tynames $E$ may not contain all the type names which have been generated; one reason is that a context $T, \emptyset, E$ is a projection of the basis $B = T, F, G, E$ whose other components $F$ and $G$ could contain other such names – recorded in $T$ but not present in $E$. Of course, remarks about what "has been generated" are not precise in terms of the semantic rules. But the following precise result may easily be demonstrated:

> Let S be a sentence $T, U, E \vdash phrase \Rightarrow A$ such that tynames $E \subseteq T$, and let S' be a sentence $T', U', E' \vdash phrase' \Rightarrow A'$ occurring in a proof of S; then also tynames $E' \subseteq T'$.

## Atomic Expressions $\boxed{C \vdash atexp \Rightarrow \tau}$

$$\frac{}{C \vdash scon \Rightarrow \mathrm{type}(scon)} \tag{1}$$

$$\frac{C(longvid) = (\sigma, is) \qquad \sigma \succ \tau}{C \vdash longvid \Rightarrow \tau} \tag{2}$$

$$\frac{\langle C \vdash exprow \Rightarrow \varrho \rangle}{C \vdash \{ \; \langle exprow \rangle \; \} \Rightarrow \{\}\langle + \varrho \rangle \; \text{in Type}} \tag{3}$$

$$\frac{C \vdash dec \Rightarrow E \qquad C \oplus E \vdash exp \Rightarrow \tau \qquad \text{tynames} \, \tau \subseteq T \, \text{of} \, C}{C \vdash \texttt{let} \; dec \; \texttt{in} \; exp \; \texttt{end} \Rightarrow \tau} \tag{4}$$

$$\frac{C \vdash exp \Rightarrow \tau}{C \vdash ( \; exp \; ) \Rightarrow \tau} \tag{5}$$

*Comments:*

(2) The instantiation of type schemes allows different occurrences of a single *longvid* to assume different types. Note that the identifier status is not used in this rule.

(4) The use of $\oplus$, here and elsewhere, ensures that type names generated by the first sub-phrase are different from type names generated by the second sub-phrase. The side condition prevents type names generated by *dec* from escaping outside the local declaration.

## Expression Rows $\boxed{C \vdash exprow \Rightarrow \varrho}$

$$\frac{C \vdash exp \Rightarrow \tau \qquad \langle C \vdash exprow \Rightarrow \varrho\rangle}{C \vdash lab = exp \langle\, ,\ exprow\rangle \Rightarrow \{lab \mapsto \tau\}\langle + \varrho\rangle} \tag{6}$$

## Expressions $\boxed{C \vdash exp \Rightarrow \tau}$

$$\frac{C \vdash atexp \Rightarrow \tau}{C \vdash atexp \Rightarrow \tau} \tag{7}$$

$$\frac{C \vdash exp \Rightarrow \tau' \to \tau \qquad C \vdash atexp \Rightarrow \tau'}{C \vdash exp\ atexp \Rightarrow \tau} \tag{8}$$

$$\frac{C \vdash exp \Rightarrow \tau \qquad C \vdash ty \Rightarrow \tau}{C \vdash exp\ :\ ty \Rightarrow \tau} \tag{9}$$

$$\frac{C \vdash exp \Rightarrow \tau \qquad C \vdash match \Rightarrow \mathbf{exn} \to \tau}{C \vdash exp\ \mathtt{handle}\ match \Rightarrow \tau} \tag{10}$$

$$\frac{C \vdash exp \Rightarrow \mathbf{exn}}{C \vdash \mathtt{raise}\ exp \Rightarrow \tau} \tag{11}$$

$$\frac{C \vdash match \Rightarrow \tau}{C \vdash \mathtt{fn}\ match \Rightarrow \tau} \tag{12}$$

*Comments:*

(7) The relational symbol $\vdash$ is overloaded for all syntactic classes (here atomic expressions and expressions).

(9) Here $\tau$ is determined by $C$ and *ty*. Notice that type variables in *ty* cannot be instantiated in obtaining $\tau$; thus the expression `1:'a` will not elaborate successfully, nor will the expression `(fn x=>x):'a->'b`. The effect of type variables in an explicitly typed expression is to indicate exactly the degree of polymorphism present in the expression.

(11) Note that $\tau$ does not occur in the premise; thus a `raise` expression has "arbitrary" type.

## Matches $\boxed{C \vdash match \Rightarrow \tau}$

$$\frac{C \vdash mrule \Rightarrow \tau \qquad \langle C \vdash match \Rightarrow \tau\rangle}{C \vdash mrule \langle\ |\ match\rangle \Rightarrow \tau} \tag{13}$$

## Match Rules

$$\boxed{C \vdash mrule \Rightarrow \tau}$$

$$\frac{C \vdash pat \Rightarrow (VE, \tau) \qquad C + VE \vdash exp \Rightarrow \tau' \qquad \text{tynames } VE \subseteq T \text{ of } C}{C \vdash pat \texttt{ => } exp \Rightarrow \tau \rightarrow \tau'} \tag{14}$$

*Comment:* This rule allows new free type variables to enter the context. These new type variables will be chosen, in effect, during the elaboration of *pat* (i.e., in the inference of the first hypothesis). In particular, their choice may have to be made to agree with type variables present in any explicit type expression occurring within *exp* (see rule 9).

## Declarations

$$\boxed{C \vdash dec \Rightarrow E}$$

$$\frac{U = \text{tyvars}(tyvarseq) \\ C + U \vdash valbind \Rightarrow VE \qquad VE' = \text{Clos}_{C,valbind} VE \qquad U \cap \text{tyvars } VE' = \emptyset}{C \vdash \texttt{val } tyvarseq \; valbind \Rightarrow VE' \text{ in Env}} \tag{15}$$

$$\frac{C \vdash typbind \Rightarrow TE}{C \vdash \texttt{type } typbind \Rightarrow TE \text{ in Env}} \tag{16}$$

$$\frac{C \oplus TE \vdash datbind \Rightarrow VE, TE \qquad \forall (t, VE') \in \text{Ran } TE, \; t \notin (T \text{ of } C) \\ TE \text{ maximises equality}}{C \vdash \texttt{datatype } datbind \Rightarrow (VE, TE) \text{ in Env}} \tag{17}$$

$$\frac{C(longtycon) = (\theta, VE) \qquad TE = \{tycon \mapsto (\theta, VE)\}}{C \vdash \texttt{datatype } tycon \texttt{ = datatype } longtycon \Rightarrow (VE, TE) \text{ in Env}} \tag{18}$$

$$\frac{C \oplus TE \vdash datbind \Rightarrow VE, TE \qquad \forall (t, VE') \in \text{Ran } TE, \; t \notin (T \text{ of } C) \\ C \oplus (VE, TE) \vdash dec \Rightarrow E \qquad TE \text{ maximises equality}}{C \vdash \texttt{abstype } datbind \texttt{ with } dec \texttt{ end} \Rightarrow \text{Abs}(TE, E)} \tag{19}$$

$$\frac{C \vdash exbind \Rightarrow VE}{C \vdash \texttt{exception } exbind \Rightarrow VE \text{ in Env}} \tag{20}$$

$$\frac{C \vdash dec_1 \Rightarrow E_1 \qquad C \oplus E_1 \vdash dec_2 \Rightarrow E_2}{C \vdash \texttt{local } dec_1 \texttt{ in } dec_2 \texttt{ end} \Rightarrow E_2} \tag{21}$$

$$\frac{C(longstrid_1) = E_1 \quad \cdots \quad C(longstrid_n) = E_n}{C \vdash \texttt{open } longstrid_1 \cdots longstrid_n \Rightarrow E_1 + \cdots + E_n} \tag{22}$$

$$\frac{}{C \vdash \quad \Rightarrow \{\} \text{ in Env}} \tag{23}$$

$$\frac{C \vdash dec_1 \Rightarrow E_1 \qquad C \oplus E_1 \vdash dec_2 \Rightarrow E_2}{C \vdash dec_1 \; \langle ; \rangle \; dec_2 \Rightarrow E_1 + E_2} \tag{24}$$

*Comments:*

(15) Here $VE$ will contain types rather than general type schemes. The closure of $VE$ allows value identifiers to be used polymorphically, via rule 2.

The side-condition on $U$ ensures that the type variables in *tyvarseq* are bound by the closure operation, if they occur free in the range of $VE$.

On the other hand, if the phrase **val** *tyvarseq valbind* occurs inside some larger value binding **val** *tyvarseq′ valbind′* then no type variable $\alpha$ listed in *tyvarseq′* will become bound by the $\text{Clos}_{C,valbind} VE$ operation; for $\alpha$ must be in $U$ of $C$ and hence excluded from closure by the definition of the closure operation (Section 4.8, page 20) since $U$ of $C \subseteq \text{tyvars}\, C$.

(17),(19) The side conditions express that the elaboration of each datatype binding generates new type names and that as many of these new names as possible admit equality. Adding $TE$ to the context on the left of the $\vdash$ captures the recursive nature of the binding.

(18) Note that no new type name is generated (i.e., datatype replication is not generative).

(19) The Abs operation was defined in Section 4.9, page 20.

(20) No closure operation is used here, as this would make the type system unsound. Example: `exception E of 'a; val it = (raise E 5) handle E f => f(2)` .

## Value Bindings                                   $\boxed{C \vdash valbind \Rightarrow VE}$

$$\frac{C \vdash pat \Rightarrow (VE, \tau) \qquad C \vdash exp \Rightarrow \tau \qquad \langle C \vdash valbind \Rightarrow VE′ \rangle}{C \vdash pat = exp \; \langle \textbf{and} \; valbind \rangle \Rightarrow VE \; \langle + \; VE′ \rangle} \tag{25}$$

$$\frac{C + VE \vdash valbind \Rightarrow VE \qquad \text{tynames}\, VE \subseteq T \text{ of } C}{C \vdash \textbf{rec} \; valbind \Rightarrow VE} \tag{26}$$

*Comments:*

(25) When the option is present we have $\text{Dom}\, VE \cap \text{Dom}\, VE′ = \emptyset$ by the syntactic restrictions.

(26) Modifying $C$ by $VE$ on the left captures the recursive nature of the binding. From rule 25 we see that any type scheme occurring in $VE$ will have to be a type. Thus each use of a recursive function in its own body must be assigned the same type. Also note that $C + VE$ may overwrite identifier status. For example, the program `datatype t = f; val rec f = fn x => x;`   is legal.

## Type Bindings $\boxed{C \vdash \mathit{typbind} \Rightarrow TE}$

$$\frac{\mathit{tyvarseq} = \alpha^{(k)} \qquad C \vdash \mathit{ty} \Rightarrow \tau \qquad \langle C \vdash \mathit{typbind} \Rightarrow TE \rangle}{\begin{array}{c} C \vdash \mathit{tyvarseq\ tycon} \texttt{ = } \mathit{ty}\ \langle \texttt{and}\ \mathit{typbind} \rangle \Rightarrow \\ \{\mathit{tycon} \mapsto (\Lambda \alpha^{(k)}.\tau, \{\})\}\ \langle + TE \rangle \end{array}} \tag{27}$$

*Comment:* The syntactic restrictions ensure that the type function $\Lambda \alpha^{(k)}.\tau$ satisfies the well-formedness constraint of Section 4.4 and they ensure $\mathit{tycon} \notin \mathrm{Dom}\, TE$.

## Datatype Bindings $\boxed{C \vdash \mathit{datbind} \Rightarrow VE, TE}$

$$\frac{\begin{array}{c} \mathit{tyvarseq} = \alpha^{(k)} \qquad C, \alpha^{(k)} t \vdash \mathit{conbind} \Rightarrow VE \qquad \mathrm{arity}\, t = k \\ \langle C \vdash \mathit{datbind}' \Rightarrow VE', TE' \qquad \forall (t', VE'') \in \mathrm{Ran}\, TE', t \neq t' \rangle \end{array}}{\begin{array}{c} C \vdash \mathit{tyvarseq\ tycon} \texttt{ = } \mathit{conbind}\ \langle \texttt{and}\ \mathit{datbind}' \rangle \Rightarrow \\ (\mathrm{Clos}\, VE \langle + VE' \rangle, \{\mathit{tycon} \mapsto (t, \mathrm{Clos}\, VE)\}\ \langle + TE' \rangle \end{array}} \tag{28}$$

*Comment:* The syntactic restrictions ensure $\mathrm{Dom}\, VE \cap \mathrm{Dom}\, VE' = \emptyset$ and $\mathit{tycon} \notin \mathrm{Dom}\, TE'$.

## Constructor Bindings $\boxed{C, \tau \vdash \mathit{conbind} \Rightarrow VE}$

$$\frac{\langle C \vdash \mathit{ty} \Rightarrow \tau' \rangle \qquad \langle\langle C, \tau \vdash \mathit{conbind} \Rightarrow VE \rangle\rangle}{\begin{array}{c} C, \tau \vdash \mathit{vid}\ \langle \texttt{of}\ \mathit{ty} \rangle\ \langle\langle\ \texttt{|}\ \mathit{conbind} \rangle\rangle \Rightarrow \\ \{\mathit{vid} \mapsto (\tau, \mathtt{c})\}\ \langle + \{\mathit{vid} \mapsto (\tau' \to \tau, \mathtt{c})\}\ \rangle\ \langle\langle + VE \rangle\rangle \end{array}} \tag{29}$$

*Comment:* By the syntactic restrictions $\mathit{vid} \notin \mathrm{Dom}\, VE$.

## Exception Bindings $\boxed{C \vdash \mathit{exbind} \Rightarrow VE}$

$$\frac{\langle C \vdash \mathit{ty} \Rightarrow \tau \rangle \qquad \langle\langle C \vdash \mathit{exbind} \Rightarrow VE \rangle\rangle}{\begin{array}{c} C \vdash \mathit{vid}\ \langle \texttt{of}\ \mathit{ty} \rangle\ \langle\langle \texttt{and}\ \mathit{exbind} \rangle\rangle \Rightarrow \\ \{\mathit{vid} \mapsto (\mathtt{exn}, \mathtt{e})\}\ \langle + \{\mathit{vid} \mapsto (\tau \to \mathtt{exn}, \mathtt{e})\}\ \rangle\ \langle\langle + VE \rangle\rangle \end{array}} \tag{30}$$

$$\frac{C(\mathit{longvid}) = (\tau, \mathtt{e}) \qquad \langle C \vdash \mathit{exbind} \Rightarrow VE \rangle}{C \vdash \mathit{vid} \texttt{ = } \mathit{longvid}\ \langle \texttt{and}\ \mathit{exbind} \rangle \Rightarrow \{\mathit{vid} \mapsto (\tau, \mathtt{e})\}\ \langle + VE \rangle} \tag{31}$$

*Comments:*

(30) Notice that $\tau$ may contain type variables.

(30),(31) For each $C$ and *exbind*, there is at most one $VE$ satisfying $C \vdash \mathit{exbind} \Rightarrow VE$.

**Atomic Patterns**                                         $\boxed{C \vdash atpat \Rightarrow (VE, \tau)}$

$$\overline{C \vdash \_ \Rightarrow (\{\}, \tau)} \tag{32}$$

$$\overline{C \vdash scon \Rightarrow (\{\}, \text{type}(scon))} \tag{33}$$

$$\frac{vid \notin \text{Dom}(C) \text{ or } is \text{ of } C(vid) = \mathbf{v}}{C \vdash vid \Rightarrow (\{vid \mapsto (\tau, \mathbf{v})\}, \tau)} \tag{34}$$

$$\frac{C(longvid) = (\sigma, is) \qquad is \neq \mathbf{v} \qquad \sigma \succ \tau^{(k)}t}{C \vdash longvid \Rightarrow (\{\}, \tau^{(k)}t)} \tag{35}$$

$$\frac{\langle C \vdash patrow \Rightarrow (VE, \varrho) \rangle}{C \vdash \{ \langle patrow \rangle \} \Rightarrow ( \{\}\langle + VE \rangle, \{\}\langle + \varrho \rangle \text{ in Type })} \tag{36}$$

$$\frac{C \vdash pat \Rightarrow (VE, \tau)}{C \vdash ( pat ) \Rightarrow (VE, \tau)} \tag{37}$$

*Comments:*

(34), (35) The context $C$ determines which of these two rules applies. In rule 34, note that *vid* can assume a type, not a general type scheme.

**Pattern Rows**                                           $\boxed{C \vdash patrow \Rightarrow (VE, \varrho)}$

$$\overline{C \vdash \ldots \Rightarrow (\{\}, \varrho)} \tag{38}$$

$$\frac{C \vdash pat \Rightarrow (VE, \tau) \qquad \langle C \vdash patrow \Rightarrow (VE', \varrho) \qquad \text{Dom } VE \cap \text{Dom } VE' = \emptyset \rangle}{C \vdash lab = pat \langle \, , patrow \rangle \Rightarrow (VE\langle + VE' \rangle, \{lab \mapsto \tau\}\langle + \varrho \rangle)} \tag{39}$$

*Comment:*

(39) The syntactic restrictions ensure $lab \notin \text{Dom } \varrho$.

**Patterns**                                               $\boxed{C \vdash pat \Rightarrow (VE, \tau)}$

$$\frac{C \vdash atpat \Rightarrow (VE, \tau)}{C \vdash atpat \Rightarrow (VE, \tau)} \tag{40}$$

$$\frac{C(longvid) = (\sigma, is) \qquad is \neq \mathbf{v} \qquad \sigma \succ \tau' \to \tau \qquad C \vdash atpat \Rightarrow (VE, \tau')}{C \vdash longvid \ atpat \Rightarrow (VE, \tau)} \tag{41}$$

$$\frac{C \vdash pat \Rightarrow (VE, \tau) \qquad C \vdash ty \Rightarrow \tau}{C \vdash pat : ty \Rightarrow (VE, \tau)} \tag{42}$$

$$\frac{\begin{array}{c} vid \notin \mathrm{Dom}(C) \text{ or } is \text{ of } C(vid) = \mathbf{v} \\ \langle C \vdash ty \Rightarrow \tau \rangle \qquad C \vdash pat \Rightarrow (VE, \tau) \qquad vid \notin \mathrm{Dom}\, VE \end{array}}{C \vdash vid\langle : ty\rangle \text{ as } pat \Rightarrow (\{vid \mapsto (\tau, \mathbf{v})\} + VE, \tau)} \tag{43}$$

## Type Expressions $\boxed{C \vdash ty \Rightarrow \tau}$

$$\frac{tyvar = \alpha}{C \vdash tyvar \Rightarrow \alpha} \tag{44}$$

$$\frac{\langle C \vdash tyrow \Rightarrow \varrho \rangle}{C \vdash \{ \langle tyrow \rangle \} \Rightarrow \{\}\langle + \varrho\rangle \text{ in Type}} \tag{45}$$

$$\frac{\begin{array}{c} tyseq = ty_1 \cdots ty_k \qquad C \vdash ty_i \Rightarrow \tau_i \ (1 \le i \le k) \\ C(longtycon) = (\theta, VE) \end{array}}{C \vdash tyseq \ longtycon \Rightarrow \tau^{(k)}\theta} \tag{46}$$

$$\frac{C \vdash ty \Rightarrow \tau \qquad C \vdash ty' \Rightarrow \tau'}{C \vdash ty \text{ -> } ty' \Rightarrow \tau \to \tau'} \tag{47}$$

$$\frac{C \vdash ty \Rightarrow \tau}{C \vdash ( \, ty \, ) \Rightarrow \tau} \tag{48}$$

*Comments:*

(46) Recall that for $\tau^{(k)}\theta$ to be defined, $\theta$ must have arity $k$.

## Type-expression Rows $\boxed{C \vdash tyrow \Rightarrow \varrho}$

$$\frac{C \vdash ty \Rightarrow \tau \qquad \langle C \vdash tyrow \Rightarrow \varrho \rangle}{C \vdash lab : ty \, \langle \, , tyrow\rangle \Rightarrow \{lab \mapsto \tau\}\langle + \varrho\rangle} \tag{49}$$

*Comment:* The syntactic constraints ensure $lab \notin \mathrm{Dom}\, \varrho$.

## 4.11   Further Restrictions

There are a few restrictions on programs which should be enforced by a compiler, but are better expressed apart from the preceding Inference Rules. They are:

1. For each occurrence of a record pattern containing a record wildcard, i.e. of the form $\{lab_1 \texttt{=} pat_1, \cdots, lab_m \texttt{=} pat_m, \ldots\}$ the program context must determine uniquely the domain $\{lab_1, \cdots, lab_n\}$ of its row type, where $m \le n$; thus, the context must determine the labels $\{lab_{m+1}, \cdots, lab_n\}$ of the fields to be matched by the wildcard. For this purpose, an explicit type constraint may be needed.

2. In a match of the form $pat_1$ => $exp_1$ | $\cdots$ | $pat_n$ => $exp_n$ the pattern sequence $pat_1, \ldots, pat_n$ should be *irredundant*; that is, each $pat_j$ must match some value (of the right type) which is not matched by $pat_i$ for any $i < j$. In the context **fn** *match*, the *match* must also be *exhaustive*; that is, every value (of the right type) must be matched by some $pat_i$. The compiler must give warning on violation of these restrictions, but should still compile the match. The restrictions are inherited by derived forms; in particular, this means that in the function-value binding *vid* $atpat_1 \cdots atpat_n \langle: ty \rangle$ = *exp* (consisting of one clause only), each separate $atpat_i$ should be exhaustive by itself.

3. For each value binding *pat* = *exp* the compiler must issue a report (but still compile) if *pat* is not exhaustive. This will detect a mistaken declaration like **val nil** = *exp* in which the user expects to declare a new variable **nil** (whereas the language dictates that **nil** is here a constant pattern, so no variable gets declared). However, this warning should not be given when the binding is a component of a top-level declaration **val** *valbind*; e.g. **val x::1** = $exp_1$ and **y** = $exp_2$ is not faulted by the compiler at top level, but may of course generate a Bind exception (see Section 6.5).

# 5 Static Semantics for Modules

## 5.1 Semantic Objects

The simple objects for Modules static semantics are exactly as for the Core. The compound objects are those for the Core, augmented by those in Figure 11.

$$
\begin{aligned}
\Sigma \text{ or } (T)E &\in \text{Sig} = \text{TyNameSet} \times \text{Env} \\
\Phi \text{ or } (T)(E,(T')E') &\in \text{FunSig} = \text{TyNameSet} \times (\text{Env} \times \text{Sig}) \\
G &\in \text{SigEnv} = \text{SigId} \overset{\text{fin}}{\to} \text{Sig} \\
F &\in \text{FunEnv} = \text{FunId} \overset{\text{fin}}{\to} \text{FunSig} \\
B \text{ or } T,F,G,E &\in \text{Basis} = \text{TyNameSet} \times \text{FunEnv} \times \text{SigEnv} \times \text{Env}
\end{aligned}
$$

Figure 11: Further Compound Semantic Objects

The prefix $(T)$, in signatures and functor signatures, binds type names. Certain operations require a change of bound names in semantic objects; see for example Section 5.2. When bound type names are changed, we demand that all of their attributes (i.e. equality and arity) are preserved.

The operations of projection, injection and modification are as for the Core. Moreover, we define $C$ of $B$ to be the context $(T \text{ of } B, \emptyset, E \text{ of } B)$, i.e. with an empty set of explicit type variables. Also, we frequently need to modify a basis $B$ by an environment $E$ (or a structure environment $SE$ say), at the same time extending $T$ of $B$ to include the type names of $E$ (or of $SE$ say). We therefore define $B \oplus SE$, for example, to mean $B + (\text{tynames } SE, SE)$.

There is no separate kind of semantic object to represent structures: structure expressions elaborate to environments, just as structure-level declarations do. Thus, notions which are commonly associated with structures (for example the notion of matching a structure against a signature) are defined in terms of environments.

## 5.2 Type Realisation

A *(type) realisation* is a map $\varphi : \text{TyName} \to \text{TypeFcn}$ such that $t$ and $\varphi(t)$ have the same arity, and if $t$ admits equality then so does $\varphi(t)$.

The *support* $\text{Supp}\,\varphi$ of a type realisation $\varphi$ is the set of type names $t$ for which $\varphi(t) \neq t$. The *yield* $\text{Yield}\,\varphi$ of a realisation $\varphi$ is the set of type names which occur in some $\varphi(t)$ for which $t \in \text{Supp}\,\varphi$.

Realisations $\varphi$ are extended to apply to all semantic objects; their effect is to replace each name $t$ by $\varphi(t)$. In applying $\varphi$ to an object with bound names, such as a signature $(T)E$, first bound names must be changed so that, for each binding prefix $(T)$,

$$
T \cap (\text{Supp}\,\varphi \cup \text{Yield}\,\varphi) = \emptyset \ .
$$

## 5.3  Signature Instantiation

An environment $E_2$ *is an instance of* a signature $\Sigma_1 = (T_1)E_1$, written $\Sigma_1 \geq E_2$, if there exists a realisation $\varphi$ such that $\varphi(E_1) = E_2$ and $\operatorname{Supp} \varphi \subseteq T_1$.

## 5.4  Functor Signature Instantiation

A pair $(E, (T')E')$ is called a *functor instance*. Given $\Phi = (T_1)(E_1, (T_1')E_1')$, a functor instance $(E_2, (T_2')E_2')$ is an *instance of* $\Phi$, written $\Phi \geq (E_2, (T_2')E_2')$, if there exists a realisation $\varphi$ such that $\varphi(E_1, (T_1')E_1') = (E_2, (T_2')E_2')$ and $\operatorname{Supp} \varphi \subseteq T_1$.

## 5.5  Enrichment

In matching an environment to a signature, the environment will be allowed both to have more components, and to be more polymorphic, than (an instance of) the signature. Precisely, we define enrichment of environments and type structures recursively as follows.

An environment $E_1 = (SE_1, TE_1, VE_1)$ *enriches* another environment $E_2 = (SE_2, TE_2, VE_2)$, written $E_1 \succ E_2$, if

1. $\operatorname{Dom} SE_1 \supseteq \operatorname{Dom} SE_2$, and $SE_1(strid) \succ SE_2(strid)$ for all $strid \in \operatorname{Dom} SE_2$

2. $\operatorname{Dom} TE_1 \supseteq \operatorname{Dom} TE_2$, and $TE_1(tycon) \succ TE_2(tycon)$ for all $tycon \in \operatorname{Dom} TE_2$

3. $\operatorname{Dom} VE_1 \supseteq \operatorname{Dom} VE_2$, and $VE_1(vid) \succ VE_2(vid)$ for all $vid \in \operatorname{Dom} VE_2$, where $(\sigma_1, is_1) \succ (\sigma_2, is_2)$ means $\sigma_1 \succ \sigma_2$ and

$$is_1 = is_2 \quad \text{or} \quad is_2 = \mathbf{v}$$

Finally, a type structure $(\theta_1, VE_1)$ *enriches* another type structure $(\theta_2, VE_2)$, written $(\theta_1, VE_1) \succ (\theta_2, VE_2)$, if

1. $\theta_1 = \theta_2$

2. Either $VE_1 = VE_2$ or $VE_2 = \{\}$

## 5.6  Signature Matching

An environment $E$ *matches* a signature $\Sigma_1$ if there exists an environment $E^-$ such that $\Sigma_1 \geq E^- \prec E$. Thus matching is a combination of instantiation and enrichment. There is at most one such $E^-$, given $\Sigma_1$ and $E$.

## 5.7   Inference Rules

As for the Core, the rules of the Modules static semantics allow sentences of the form

$$A \vdash phrase \Rightarrow A'$$

to be inferred, where in this case $A$ is either a basis, a context or an environment and $A'$ is a semantic object. The convention for options is as in the Core semantics.

   Although not assumed in our definitions, it is intended that every basis $B = T, F, G, E$ in which a *topdec* is elaborated has the property that tynames $F \cup$ tynames $G \cup$ tynames $E \subseteq T$. The following Theorem can be proved:

> Let S be an inferred sentence $B \vdash topdec \Rightarrow B'$ in which $B$ satisfies the above condition. Then $B'$ also satisfies the condition.
>
> Moreover, if $S'$ is a sentence of the form $B'' \vdash phrase \Rightarrow A$ occurring in a proof of S, where *phrase* is any Modules phrase, then $B''$ also satisfies the condition.
>
> Finally, if $T, U, E \vdash phrase \Rightarrow A$ occurs in a proof of S, where *phrase* is a phrase of Modules or of the Core, then tynames $E \subseteq T$.

### Structure Expressions $\boxed{B \vdash strexp \Rightarrow E}$

$$\frac{B \vdash strdec \Rightarrow E}{B \vdash \texttt{struct}\ strdec\ \texttt{end} \Rightarrow E} \tag{50}$$

$$\frac{B(longstrid) = E}{B \vdash longstrid \Rightarrow E} \tag{51}$$

$$\frac{B \vdash strexp \Rightarrow E \quad B \vdash sigexp \Rightarrow \Sigma \quad \Sigma \geq E' \prec E}{B \vdash strexp : sigexp \Rightarrow E'} \tag{52}$$

$$\frac{\begin{array}{c} B \vdash strexp \Rightarrow E \quad B \vdash sigexp \Rightarrow (T')E' \\ (T')E' \geq E'' \prec E \quad T' \cap (T \text{ of } B) = \emptyset \end{array}}{B \vdash strexp :> sigexp \Rightarrow E'} \tag{53}$$

$$\frac{\begin{array}{c} B \vdash strexp \Rightarrow E \\ B(funid) \geq (E'', (T')E') , \ E \succ E'' \\ (\text{tynames } E \ \cup \ T \text{ of } B) \cap T' = \emptyset \end{array}}{B \vdash funid\ (\ strexp\ ) \ \Rightarrow E'} \tag{54}$$

$$\frac{B \vdash strdec \Rightarrow E_1 \quad B \oplus E_1 \vdash strexp \Rightarrow E_2}{B \vdash \texttt{let}\ strdec\ \texttt{in}\ strexp\ \texttt{end} \Rightarrow E_2} \tag{55}$$

*Comments:*

(54) The side condition (tynames $E \cup T$ of $B$) $\cap T' = \emptyset$ can always be satisfied by renaming bound names in $(T')E'$; it ensures that the generated datatypes receive new names.

Let $B(funid) = (T)(E_f, (T')E_f')$. Let $\varphi$ be a realisation such that $\varphi(E_f, (T')E_f') = (E'', (T')E')$. Sharing between argument and result specified in the declaration of the functor *funid* is represented by the occurrence of the same name in both $E_f$ and $E_f'$, and this repeated occurrence is preserved by $\varphi$, yielding sharing between the argument structure $E$ and the result structure $E'$ of this functor application.

(55) The use of $\oplus$, here and elsewhere, ensures that type names generated by the first sub-phrase are distinct from names generated by the second sub-phrase.

## Structure-level Declarations                    $\boxed{B \vdash strdec \Rightarrow E}$

$$\frac{C \text{ of } B \vdash dec \Rightarrow E}{B \vdash dec \Rightarrow E} \tag{56}$$

$$\frac{B \vdash strbind \Rightarrow SE}{B \vdash \texttt{structure } strbind \Rightarrow SE \text{ in Env}} \tag{57}$$

$$\frac{B \vdash strdec_1 \Rightarrow E_1 \qquad B \oplus E_1 \vdash strdec_2 \Rightarrow E_2}{B \vdash \texttt{local } strdec_1 \texttt{ in } strdec_2 \texttt{ end} \Rightarrow E_2} \tag{58}$$

$$\frac{}{B \vdash \quad \Rightarrow \{\} \text{ in Env}} \tag{59}$$

$$\frac{B \vdash strdec_1 \Rightarrow E_1 \qquad B \oplus E_1 \vdash strdec_2 \Rightarrow E_2}{B \vdash strdec_1 \langle; \rangle strdec_2 \Rightarrow E_1 + E_2} \tag{60}$$

## Structure Bindings                              $\boxed{B \vdash strbind \Rightarrow SE}$

$$\frac{B \vdash strexp \Rightarrow E \quad \langle B + \text{tynames } E \vdash strbind \Rightarrow SE \rangle}{B \vdash strid \texttt{ = } strexp \; \langle \texttt{and } strbind \rangle \Rightarrow \{strid \mapsto E\} \langle + \; SE \rangle} \tag{61}$$

## Signature Expressions                           $\boxed{B \vdash sigexp \Rightarrow E}$

$$\frac{B \vdash spec \Rightarrow E}{B \vdash \texttt{sig } spec \texttt{ end} \Rightarrow E} \tag{62}$$

$$\frac{B(sigid) = (T)E \quad T \cap (T \text{ of } B) = \emptyset}{B \vdash sigid \Rightarrow E} \tag{63}$$

$$\frac{\begin{array}{c} B \vdash sigexp \Rightarrow E \quad tyvarseq = \alpha^{(k)} \quad C \text{ of } B \vdash ty \Rightarrow \tau \\ E(longtycon) = (t, VE) \quad t \notin T \text{ of } B \\ \varphi = \{t \mapsto \Lambda\alpha^{(k)}.\tau\} \quad \Lambda\alpha^{(k)}.\tau \text{ admits equality, if } t \text{ does} \quad \varphi(E) \text{ well-formed} \end{array}}{B \vdash sigexp \text{ where type } tyvarseq \; longtycon \; \texttt{=} \; ty \Rightarrow \varphi(E)} \tag{64}$$

*Comments:*

(63) The bound names of $B(sigid)$ can always be renamed to satisfy $T \cap (T \text{ of } B) = \emptyset$, if necessary.

$$\boxed{B \vdash sigexp \Rightarrow \Sigma}$$

$$\frac{B \vdash sigexp \Rightarrow E \quad T = \text{tynames } E \setminus (T \text{ of } B)}{B \vdash sigexp \Rightarrow (T)E} \tag{65}$$

*Comment:* A signature expression *sigexp* which is an immediate constituent of a signature binding, a signature constraint, or a functor binding is elaborated to a signature, see rules 52, 53, 67 and 86.

## Signature Declarations $\qquad\boxed{B \vdash sigdec \Rightarrow G}$

$$\frac{B \vdash sigbind \Rightarrow G}{B \vdash \texttt{signature } sigbind \Rightarrow G} \tag{66}$$

## Signature Bindings $\qquad\boxed{B \vdash sigbind \Rightarrow G}$

$$\frac{B \vdash sigexp \Rightarrow \Sigma \quad \langle B \vdash sigbind \Rightarrow G\rangle}{B \vdash sigid \texttt{ = } sigexp \langle\texttt{and } sigbind\rangle \Rightarrow \{sigid \mapsto \Sigma\} \langle+ \; G\rangle} \tag{67}$$

## Specifications $\qquad\boxed{B \vdash spec \Rightarrow E}$

$$\frac{C \text{ of } B \vdash valdesc \Rightarrow VE}{B \vdash \texttt{val } valdesc \Rightarrow \text{Clos} VE \text{ in Env}} \tag{68}$$

$$\frac{C \text{ of } B \vdash typdesc \Rightarrow TE \quad \forall(t, VE) \in \text{Ran } TE, \; t \text{ does not admit equality}}{B \vdash \texttt{type } typdesc \Rightarrow TE \text{ in Env}} \tag{69}$$

$$\frac{C \text{ of } B \vdash typdesc \Rightarrow TE \quad \forall(t, VE) \in \text{Ran } TE, \; t \text{ admits equality}}{B \vdash \texttt{eqtype } typdesc \Rightarrow TE \text{ in Env}} \tag{70}$$

$$\frac{\begin{array}{cc} C \text{ of } B \oplus TE \vdash datdesc \Rightarrow VE, TE & \forall (t, VE') \in \text{Ran } TE, t \notin T \text{ of } B \\ \multicolumn{2}{c}{TE \text{ maximises equality}} \end{array}}{B \vdash \texttt{datatype } datdesc \Rightarrow (VE, TE) \text{ in Env}} \tag{71}$$

$$\frac{B(longtycon) = (\theta, VE) \qquad TE = \{tycon \mapsto (\theta, VE)\}}{B \vdash \texttt{datatype } tycon \texttt{ = datatype } longtycon \Rightarrow (VE, TE) \text{ in Env}} \tag{72}$$

$$\frac{C \text{ of } B \vdash exdesc \Rightarrow VE}{B \vdash \texttt{exception } exdesc \Rightarrow VE \text{ in Env}} \tag{73}$$

$$\frac{B \vdash strdesc \Rightarrow SE}{B \vdash \texttt{structure } strdesc \Rightarrow SE \text{ in Env}} \tag{74}$$

$$\frac{B \vdash sigexp \Rightarrow E}{B \vdash \texttt{include } sigexp \Rightarrow E} \tag{75}$$

$$\frac{}{B \vdash \quad \Rightarrow \{\} \text{ in Env}} \tag{76}$$

$$\frac{B \vdash spec_1 \Rightarrow E_1 \qquad B \oplus E_1 \vdash spec_2 \Rightarrow E_2 \qquad \text{Dom}(E_1) \cap \text{Dom}(E_2) = \emptyset}{B \vdash spec_1 \ \langle ; \rangle \ spec_2 \Rightarrow E_1 + E_2} \tag{77}$$

$$\frac{\begin{array}{c} B \vdash spec \Rightarrow E \quad E(longtycon_i) = (t_i, VE_i), \ i = 1..n \\ t \in \{t_1, \ldots, t_n\} \quad t \text{ admits equality, if some } t_i \text{ does} \\ \{t_1, \ldots, t_n\} \cap T \text{ of } B = \emptyset \quad \varphi = \{t_1 \mapsto t, \ldots, t_n \mapsto t\} \end{array}}{B \vdash spec \ \texttt{sharing type } longtycon_1 \texttt{ = } \cdots \texttt{ = } longtycon_n \Rightarrow \varphi(E)} \tag{78}$$

*Comments:*

(68) $VE$ is determined by $B$ and *valdesc*.

(69)–(71) The type names in $TE$ are new.

(73) $VE$ is determined by $B$ and *exdesc* and contains monotypes only.

(77) Note that no sequential specification is allowed to specify the same identifier twice.

## Value Descriptions                                        $\boxed{C \vdash valdesc \Rightarrow VE}$

$$\frac{C \vdash ty \Rightarrow \tau \qquad \langle C \vdash valdesc \Rightarrow VE \rangle}{C \vdash vid \texttt{ : } ty \ \langle \texttt{and } valdesc \rangle \Rightarrow \{vid \mapsto (\tau, \mathrm{v})\} \ \langle + \ VE \rangle} \tag{79}$$

## Type Descriptions

$$\boxed{C \vdash typdesc \Rightarrow TE}$$

$$
\frac{\begin{array}{c} tyvarseq = \alpha^{(k)} \quad t \notin T \text{ of } C \quad \text{arity } t = k \\ \langle C \vdash typdesc \Rightarrow TE \quad t \notin \text{tynames } TE \rangle \end{array}}{C \vdash tyvarseq\ tycon\ \langle \text{and } typdesc \rangle \Rightarrow \{tycon \mapsto (t, \{\})\}\ \langle + TE \rangle} \tag{80}
$$

*Comment:* Note that the value environment in the resulting type structure must be empty. For example, `datatype s=C type t sharing type t=s` is a legal specification, but the type structure bound to `t` does not bind any value constructors.

## Datatype Descriptions

$$\boxed{C \vdash datdesc \Rightarrow VE, TE}$$

$$
\frac{\begin{array}{c} tyvarseq = \alpha^{(k)} \quad C, \alpha^{(k)} t \vdash condesc \Rightarrow VE \quad \text{arity } t = k \\ \langle C \vdash datdesc' \Rightarrow VE', TE' \quad \forall (t', VE'') \in \text{Ran } TE',\ t \neq t' \rangle \end{array}}{\begin{array}{c} C \vdash tyvarseq\ tycon = condesc\ \langle \text{and } datdesc' \rangle \Rightarrow \\ \text{Clos} VE \langle + VE' \rangle,\ \{tycon \mapsto (t, \text{Clos} VE)\}\ \langle + TE' \rangle \end{array}} \tag{81}
$$

## Constructor Descriptions

$$\boxed{C, \tau \vdash condesc \Rightarrow VE}$$

$$
\frac{\langle C \vdash ty \Rightarrow \tau' \rangle \quad \langle \langle C, \tau \vdash condesc \Rightarrow VE \rangle \rangle}{\begin{array}{c} C, \tau \vdash vid\ \langle \text{of } ty \rangle\ \langle \langle\ |\ condesc \rangle \rangle \Rightarrow \\ \{vid \mapsto (\tau, \mathtt{c})\}\ \langle + \{vid \mapsto (\tau' \to \tau, \mathtt{c})\}\ \rangle\ \langle \langle + VE \rangle \rangle \end{array}} \tag{82}
$$

## Exception Descriptions

$$\boxed{C \vdash exdesc \Rightarrow VE}$$

$$
\frac{\langle C \vdash ty \Rightarrow \tau \quad \text{tyvars}(\tau) = \emptyset \rangle \quad \langle \langle C \vdash exdesc \Rightarrow VE \rangle \rangle}{\begin{array}{c} C \vdash vid\ \langle \text{of } ty \rangle\ \langle \langle \text{and } exdesc \rangle \rangle \Rightarrow \\ \{vid \mapsto (\mathtt{exn}, \mathtt{e})\}\ \langle + \{vid \mapsto (\tau \to \mathtt{exn}, \mathtt{e})\} \rangle\ \langle \langle + VE \rangle \rangle \end{array}} \tag{83}
$$

## Structure Descriptions

$$\boxed{B \vdash strdesc \Rightarrow SE}$$

$$
\frac{B \vdash sigexp \Rightarrow E \quad \langle B + \text{tynames } E \vdash strdesc \Rightarrow SE \rangle}{B \vdash strid : sigexp\ \langle \text{and } strdesc \rangle \Rightarrow \{strid \mapsto E\}\ \langle + SE \rangle} \tag{84}
$$

## Functor Declarations

$$\boxed{B \vdash fundec \Rightarrow F}$$

$$
\frac{B \vdash funbind \Rightarrow F}{B \vdash \mathtt{functor}\ funbind \Rightarrow F} \tag{85}
$$

## Functor Bindings $\boxed{B \vdash funbind \Rightarrow F}$

$$\frac{\begin{array}{cc} B \vdash sigexp \Rightarrow (T)E & B \oplus \{strid \mapsto E\} \vdash strexp \Rightarrow E' \\ T \cap (T \text{ of } B) = \emptyset & T' = \text{tynames } E' \setminus ((T \text{ of } B) \cup T) \\ \multicolumn{2}{c}{\langle B \vdash funbind \Rightarrow F \rangle} \end{array}}{\begin{array}{c} B \vdash funid\ (\ strid : sigexp\ )\ =\ strexp\ \langle \text{and}\ funbind \rangle \Rightarrow \\ \{funid \mapsto (T)(E, (T')E')\}\ \langle +\ F \rangle \end{array}} \tag{86}$$

*Comment:* Since $\oplus$ is used, any type name $t$ in $E$ acts like a constant in the functor body; in particular, it ensures that further names generated during elaboration of the body are distinct from $t$. The set $T'$ is chosen such that every name free in $(T)E$ or $(T)(E, (T')E')$ is free in $B$.

## Top-level Declarations $\boxed{B \vdash topdec \Rightarrow B'}$

$$\frac{\begin{array}{c} B \vdash strdec \Rightarrow E \quad \langle B \oplus E \vdash topdec \Rightarrow B' \rangle \\ B'' = (\text{tynames } E, E)\text{in Basis} \langle + B' \rangle \quad \text{tyvars } B'' = \emptyset \end{array}}{B \vdash strdec\ \langle topdec \rangle \Rightarrow B''} \tag{87}$$

$$\frac{\begin{array}{c} B \vdash sigdec \Rightarrow G \quad \langle B \oplus G \vdash topdec \Rightarrow B' \rangle \\ B'' = (\text{tynames } G, G) \text{ in Basis} \langle + B' \rangle \end{array}}{B \vdash sigdec\ \langle topdec \rangle \Rightarrow B''} \tag{88}$$

$$\frac{\begin{array}{c} B \vdash fundec \Rightarrow F \quad \langle B \oplus F \vdash topdec \Rightarrow B' \rangle \\ B'' = (\text{tynames } F, F) \text{ in Basis} \langle + B' \rangle \quad \text{tyvars } B'' = \emptyset \end{array}}{B \vdash fundec\ \langle topdec \rangle \Rightarrow B''} \tag{89}$$

*Comments:*

(87)–(89) No free type variables enter the basis: if $B \vdash topdec \Rightarrow B'$ then tyvars$(B') = \emptyset$.

# 6 Dynamic Semantics for the Core

## 6.1 Reduced Syntax

Since types are mostly dealt with in the static semantics, the Core syntax is reduced by the following transformations, for the purpose of the dynamic semantics:

- All explicit type ascriptions "$:\ ty$" are omitted, and qualifications "of $ty$" are omitted from constructor and exception bindings.

- The Core phrase classes Ty and TyRow are omitted.

## 6.2 Simple Objects

All objects in the dynamic semantics are built from identifier classes together with the simple object classes shown (with the variables which range over them) in Figure 12.

$$
\begin{array}{rcll}
a & \in & \text{Addr} & \text{addresses} \\
en & \in & \text{ExName} & \text{exception names} \\
b & \in & \text{BasVal} & \text{basic values} \\
sv & \in & \text{SVal} & \text{special values} \\
& & \{\text{FAIL}\} & \text{failure}
\end{array}
$$

Figure 12: Simple Semantic Objects

Addr and ExName are infinite sets. BasVal is described below. SVal is the class of values denoted by the special constants SCon. Each integer, word or real constant denotes a value according to normal mathematical conventions; each string or character constant denotes a sequence of characters as explained in Section 2.2. The value denoted by *scon* is written val(*scon*). FAIL is the result of a failing attempt to match a value and a pattern. Thus FAIL is neither a value nor an exception, but simply a semantic object used in the rules to express operationally how matching proceeds.

Exception constructors evaluate to exception names. This is to accommodate the generative nature of exception bindings; each evaluation of a declaration of a exception constructor binds it to a new unique name.

## 6.3 Compound Objects

The compound objects for the dynamic semantics are shown in Figure 13. Many conventions and notations are adopted as in the static semantics; in particular projection, injection and modification all retain their meaning. We generally omit the injection functions taking VId, VId × Val etc into Val. For records $r \in$ Record however, we write this

$$
\begin{array}{rcl}
v & \in & \mathrm{Val} = \{\,{:=}\,\} \cup \mathrm{SVal} \cup \mathrm{BasVal} \cup \mathrm{VId} \\
 & & \cup(\mathrm{VId} \times \mathrm{Val}) \cup \mathrm{ExVal} \\
 & & \cup\mathrm{Record} \cup \mathrm{Addr} \cup \mathrm{FcnClosure} \\
r & \in & \mathrm{Record} = \mathrm{Lab} \xrightarrow{\mathrm{fin}} \mathrm{Val} \\
e & \in & \mathrm{ExVal} = \mathrm{ExName} \cup (\mathrm{ExName} \times \mathrm{Val}) \\
[e]\ \mathrm{or}\ p & \in & \mathrm{Pack} = \mathrm{ExVal} \\
(match, E, VE) & \in & \mathrm{FcnClosure} = \mathrm{Match} \times \mathrm{Env} \times \mathrm{ValEnv} \\
mem & \in & \mathrm{Mem} = \mathrm{Addr} \xrightarrow{\mathrm{fin}} \mathrm{Val} \\
ens & \in & \mathrm{ExNameSet} = \mathrm{Fin}(\mathrm{ExName}) \\
(mem, ens)\ \mathrm{or}\ s & \in & \mathrm{State} = \mathrm{Mem} \times \mathrm{ExNameSet} \\
(SE, TE, VE)\ \mathrm{or}\ E & \in & \mathrm{Env} = \mathrm{StrEnv} \times \mathrm{TyEnv} \times \mathrm{ValEnv} \\
SE & \in & \mathrm{StrEnv} = \mathrm{StrId} \xrightarrow{\mathrm{fin}} \mathrm{Env} \\
TE & \in & \mathrm{TyEnv} = \mathrm{TyCon} \xrightarrow{\mathrm{fin}} \mathrm{ValEnv} \\
VE & \in & \mathrm{ValEnv} = \mathrm{VId} \xrightarrow{\mathrm{fin}} \mathrm{Val} \times \mathrm{IdStatus}
\end{array}
$$

Figure 13: Compound Semantic Objects

injection explicitly as "in Val"; this accords with the fact that there is a separate phrase class ExpRow, whose members evaluate to records.

We take $\cup$ to mean disjoint union over semantic object classes. We also understand all the defined object classes to be disjoint. A particular case deserves mention; ExVal and Pack (exception values and packets) are isomorphic classes, but the latter class corresponds to exceptions which have been raised, and therefore has different semantic significance from the former, which is just a subclass of values.

Although the same names, e.g. $E$ for an environment, are used as in the static semantics, the objects denoted are different. This need cause no confusion since the static and dynamic semantics are presented separately.

## 6.4  Basic Values

The basic values in BasVal are values bound to predefined value variables. In this document, we take BasVal to be the singleton set $\{=\}$; however, libraries may define a larger set of basic values. The meaning of basic values is represented by a function

$$
\mathrm{APPLY} \ : \ \mathrm{BasVal} \times \mathrm{Val} \to \mathrm{Val} \cup \mathrm{Pack}
$$

which satisfies that $\mathrm{APPLY}(=, \{1 \mapsto v_1, 2 \mapsto v_2\})$ is `true` or `false` according as the values $v_1$ and $v_2$ are, or are not, identical values.

## 6.5 Basic Exceptions

A subset BasExName $\subset$ ExName of the exception names are bound to predefined exception constructors in the initial dynamic basis (see Appendix D). These names are denoted by the identifiers to which they are bound in the initial basis, and are as follows:

Match   Bind

The exceptions `Match` and `Bind` are raised upon failure of pattern-matching in evaluating a function `fn` *match* or a *valbind*, as detailed in the rules to follow. Recall from Section 4.11 that in the context `fn` *match*, the *match* must be irredundant and exhaustive and that the compiler should flag the *match* if it violates these restrictions. The exception `Match` can only be raised for a match which is not exhaustive, and has therefore been flagged by the compiler.

## 6.6 Function Closures

The informal understanding of a *function closure* $(match, E, VE)$ is as follows: when the function closure is applied to a value $v$, *match* will be evaluated against $v$, in the environment $E$ modified in a special sense by $VE$. The domain Dom $VE$ of this third component contains those identifiers to be treated recursively in the evaluation. To achieve this effect, the evaluation of *match* will take place not in $E + VE$ but in $E + \text{Rec}\,VE$, where

$$\text{Rec} \;:\; \text{ValEnv} \to \text{ValEnv}$$

is defined as follows:

- $\text{Dom}(\text{Rec}\,VE) = \text{Dom}\,VE$

- If $VE(vid) \notin \text{FcnClosure} \times \{\mathbf{v}\}$, then $(\text{Rec}\,VE)(vid) = VE(vid)$

- If $VE(vid) = ((match', E', VE'), \mathbf{v})$ then $(\text{Rec}\,VE)(vid) = ((match', E', VE), \mathbf{v})$

The effect is that, before application of $(match, E, VE)$ to $v$, the function closures in Ran $VE$ are "unrolled" once, to prepare for their possible recursive application during the evaluation of *match* upon $v$.

This device is adopted to ensure that all semantic objects are finite (by controlling the unrolling of recursion). The operator Rec is invoked in just two places in the semantic rules: in the rule for recursive value bindings of the form "`rec` *valbind*", and in the rule for evaluating an application expression "*exp atexp*" in the case that *exp* evaluates to a function closure.

## 6.7   Inference Rules

The semantic rules allow sentences of the form

$$s, A \vdash phrase \Rightarrow A', s'$$

to be inferred, where $A$ is usually an environment, $A'$ is some semantic object and $s, s'$ are the states before and after the evaluation represented by the sentence. Some hypotheses in rules are not of this form; they are called *side-conditions*. The convention for options is the same as for the Core static semantics.

In most rules the states $s$ and $s'$ are omitted from sentences; they are only included for those rules which are directly concerned with the state – either referring to its contents or changing it. When omitted, the convention for restoring them is as follows. If the rule is presented in the form

$$\frac{A_1 \vdash phrase_1 \Rightarrow A_1' \qquad A_2 \vdash phrase_2 \Rightarrow A_2' \quad \cdots \quad A_n \vdash phrase_n \Rightarrow A_n'}{A \vdash phrase \Rightarrow A'}$$

then the full form is intended to be

$$\frac{s_0, A_1 \vdash phrase_1 \Rightarrow A_1', s_1 \qquad s_1, A_2 \vdash phrase_2 \Rightarrow A_2', s_2 \quad \cdots \quad s_{n-1}, A_n \vdash phrase_n \Rightarrow A_n', s_n}{s_0, A \vdash phrase \Rightarrow A', s_n}$$

(Any side-conditions are left unaltered). Thus the left-to-right order of the hypotheses indicates the order of evaluation. Note that in the case $n = 0$, when there are no hypotheses (except possibly side-conditions), we have $s_n = s_0$; this implies that the rule causes no side effect. The convention is called the *state convention*, and must be applied to each version of a rule obtained by inclusion or omission of its options.

A second convention, the *exception convention*, is adopted to deal with the propagation of exception packets $p$. For each rule whose full form (ignoring side-conditions) is

$$\frac{s_1, A_1 \vdash phrase_1 \Rightarrow A_1', s_1' \qquad \cdots \qquad s_n, A_n \vdash phrase_n \Rightarrow A_n', s_n'}{s, A \vdash phrase \Rightarrow A', s'}$$

and for each $k$, $1 \leq k \leq n$, for which the result $A_k'$ is not a packet $p$, an extra rule is added of the form

$$\frac{s_1, A_1 \vdash phrase_1 \Rightarrow A_1', s_1' \qquad \cdots \qquad s_k, A_k \vdash phrase_k \Rightarrow p', s'}{s, A \vdash phrase \Rightarrow p', s'}$$

where $p'$ does not occur in the original rule.[1] This indicates that evaluation of phrases in the hypothesis terminates with the first whose result is a packet (other than one already treated in the rule), and this packet is the result of the phrase in the conclusion.

---

[1]There is one exception to the exception convention; no extra rule is added for rule 104 which deals with handlers, since a handler is the only means by which propagation of an exception can be arrested.

A third convention is that we allow compound variables (variables built from the variables in Figure 13 and the symbol "/") to range over unions of semantic objects. For instance the compound variable $v/p$ ranges over Val $\cup$ Pack. We also allow $x$/FAIL to range over $X \cup \{\text{FAIL}\}$ where $x$ ranges over $X$; furthermore, we extend environment modification to allow for failure as follows:

$$VE + \text{FAIL} = \text{FAIL}.$$

## Atomic Expressions $\qquad\qquad\qquad\qquad \boxed{E \vdash atexp \Rightarrow v/p}$

$$\frac{}{E \vdash scon \Rightarrow \text{val}(scon)} \tag{90}$$

$$\frac{E(longvid) = (v, is)}{E \vdash longvid \Rightarrow v} \tag{91}$$

$$\frac{\langle E \vdash exprow \Rightarrow r \rangle}{E \vdash \{ \, \langle exprow \rangle \, \} \Rightarrow \{\}\langle + \, r \rangle \text{ in Val}} \tag{92}$$

$$\frac{E \vdash dec \Rightarrow E' \qquad E + E' \vdash exp \Rightarrow v}{E \vdash \texttt{let } dec \texttt{ in } exp \texttt{ end} \Rightarrow v} \tag{93}$$

$$\frac{E \vdash exp \Rightarrow v}{E \vdash ( \, exp \, ) \Rightarrow v} \tag{94}$$

*Comments:*

(91) As in the static semantics, value identifiers are looked up in the environment and the identifier status is not used.

## Expression Rows $\qquad\qquad\qquad\qquad\qquad \boxed{E \vdash exprow \Rightarrow r/p}$

$$\frac{E \vdash exp \Rightarrow v \qquad \langle E \vdash exprow \Rightarrow r \rangle}{E \vdash lab \texttt{ = } exp \, \langle \, , \, exprow \rangle \Rightarrow \{lab \mapsto v\}\langle + \, r \rangle} \tag{95}$$

*Comment:* We may think of components as being evaluated from left to right, because of the state and exception conventions.

## Expressions $\qquad\qquad\qquad\qquad\qquad\qquad \boxed{E \vdash exp \Rightarrow v/p}$

$$\frac{E \vdash atexp \Rightarrow v}{E \vdash atexp \Rightarrow v} \tag{96}$$

$$\frac{E \vdash exp \Rightarrow vid \qquad vid \neq \texttt{ref} \qquad E \vdash atexp \Rightarrow v}{E \vdash exp \; atexp \Rightarrow (vid, v)} \tag{97}$$

$$\frac{E \vdash exp \Rightarrow en \qquad E \vdash atexp \Rightarrow v}{E \vdash exp \; atexp \Rightarrow (en, v)} \tag{98}$$

$$\frac{s, E \vdash exp \Rightarrow \texttt{ref}, s' \qquad s', E \vdash atexp \Rightarrow v, s'' \qquad a \notin \mathrm{Dom}(mem \; \mathrm{of} \; s'')}{s, E \vdash exp \; atexp \Rightarrow a, \; s'' + \{a \mapsto v\}} \tag{99}$$

$$\frac{s, E \vdash exp \Rightarrow \texttt{:=}, s' \qquad s', E \vdash atexp \Rightarrow \{1 \mapsto a, \; 2 \mapsto v\}, s''}{s, E \vdash exp \; atexp \Rightarrow \{\} \; \mathrm{in} \; \mathrm{Val}, \; s'' + \{a \mapsto v\}} \tag{100}$$

$$\frac{E \vdash exp \Rightarrow b \qquad E \vdash atexp \Rightarrow v \qquad \mathrm{APPLY}(b, v) = v'/p}{E \vdash exp \; atexp \Rightarrow v'/p} \tag{101}$$

$$\frac{\begin{array}{cc} E \vdash exp \Rightarrow (match, E', VE) & E \vdash atexp \Rightarrow v \\ E' + \mathrm{Rec} \, VE, \; v \vdash match \Rightarrow v' \end{array}}{E \vdash exp \; atexp \Rightarrow v'} \tag{10?}$$

$$\frac{\begin{array}{cc} E \vdash exp \Rightarrow (match, E', VE) & E \vdash atexp \Rightarrow v \\ E' + \mathrm{Rec} \, VE, \; v \vdash match \Rightarrow \mathrm{FAIL} \end{array}}{E \vdash exp \; atexp \Rightarrow [\texttt{Match}]} \tag{103}$$

$$\frac{E \vdash exp \Rightarrow v}{E \vdash exp \; \texttt{handle} \; match \Rightarrow v} \tag{104}$$

$$\frac{E \vdash exp \Rightarrow [e] \qquad E, e \vdash match \Rightarrow v}{E \vdash exp \; \texttt{handle} \; match \Rightarrow v} \tag{105}$$

$$\frac{E \vdash exp \Rightarrow [e] \qquad E, e \vdash match \Rightarrow \mathrm{FAIL}}{E \vdash exp \; \texttt{handle} \; match \Rightarrow [e]} \tag{106}$$

$$\frac{E \vdash exp \Rightarrow e}{E \vdash \texttt{raise} \; exp \Rightarrow [e]} \tag{107}$$

$$\frac{}{E \vdash \texttt{fn} \; match \Rightarrow (match, E, \{\})} \tag{108}$$

*Comments:*

(99) The side condition ensures that a new address is chosen. There are no rules concerning disposal of inaccessible addresses.

(97)–(103) Note that none of the rules for function application has a premise in which the operator evaluates to a constructed value, a record or an address. This is because we are interested in the evaluation of well-typed programs only, and in such programs *exp* will always have a functional type.

(104) This is the only rule to which the exception convention does not apply. If the operator evaluates to a packet then rule 105 or rule 106 must be used.

(106) Packets that are not handled by the *match* propagate.

(108) The third component of the function closure is empty because the match does not introduce new recursively defined values.

## Matches

$$\boxed{E, v \vdash match \Rightarrow v'/p/\mathrm{FAIL}}$$

$$\frac{E, v \vdash mrule \Rightarrow v'}{E, v \vdash mrule \ \langle \ | \ match \rangle \Rightarrow v'} \tag{109}$$

$$\frac{E, v \vdash mrule \Rightarrow \mathrm{FAIL}}{E, v \vdash mrule \Rightarrow \mathrm{FAIL}} \tag{110}$$

$$\frac{E, v \vdash mrule \Rightarrow \mathrm{FAIL} \qquad E, v \vdash match \Rightarrow v'/\mathrm{FAIL}}{E, v \vdash mrule \ | \ match \Rightarrow v'/\mathrm{FAIL}} \tag{111}$$

*Comment:* A value $v$ occurs on the left of the turnstile, in evaluating a *match*. We may think of a *match* as being evaluated *against* a value; similarly, we may think of a pattern as being evaluated *against* a value. Alternative match rules are tried from left to right.

## Match Rules

$$\boxed{E, v \vdash mrule \Rightarrow v'/p/\mathrm{FAIL}}$$

$$\frac{E, v \vdash pat \Rightarrow VE \qquad E + VE \vdash exp \Rightarrow v'}{E, v \vdash pat \ \texttt{=>} \ exp \ \Rightarrow v'} \tag{112}$$

$$\frac{E, v \vdash pat \Rightarrow \mathrm{FAIL}}{E, v \vdash pat \ \texttt{=>} \ exp \ \Rightarrow \mathrm{FAIL}} \tag{113}$$

## Declarations

$$\boxed{E \vdash dec \Rightarrow E'/p}$$

$$\frac{E \vdash valbind \Rightarrow VE}{E \vdash \texttt{val} \ tyvarseq \ valbind \Rightarrow VE \ \text{in Env}} \tag{114}$$

$$\frac{\vdash typbind \Rightarrow TE}{E \vdash \texttt{type} \ typbind \Rightarrow TE \ \text{in Env}} \tag{115}$$

$$\frac{\vdash datbind \Rightarrow VE, TE}{E \vdash \texttt{datatype} \ datbind \Rightarrow (VE, TE) \ \text{in Env}} \tag{116}$$

$$\frac{E(longtycon) = VE}{E \vdash \texttt{datatype} \ tycon \ \texttt{=} \ \texttt{datatype} \ longtycon \Rightarrow (VE, \{tycon \mapsto VE\}) \ \text{in Env}} \tag{117}$$

$$\frac{\vdash\ datbind \Rightarrow VE, TE \qquad E + VE \vdash dec \Rightarrow E'}{E \vdash \texttt{abstype}\ datbind\ \texttt{with}\ dec\ \texttt{end} \Rightarrow E'} \tag{118}$$

$$\frac{E \vdash exbind \Rightarrow VE}{E \vdash \texttt{exception}\ exbind \Rightarrow VE\ \text{in Env}} \tag{119}$$

$$\frac{E \vdash dec_1 \Rightarrow E_1 \qquad E + E_1 \vdash dec_2 \Rightarrow E_2}{E \vdash \texttt{local}\ dec_1\ \texttt{in}\ dec_2\ \texttt{end} \Rightarrow E_2} \tag{120}$$

$$\frac{E(longstrid_1) = E_1 \quad \cdots \quad E(longstrid_n) = E_n}{E \vdash \texttt{open}\ longstrid_1\ \cdots\ longstrid_n \Rightarrow E_1 + \cdots + E_n} \tag{121}$$

$$\frac{}{E \vdash \qquad \Rightarrow \{\}\ \text{in Env}} \tag{122}$$

$$\frac{E \vdash dec_1 \Rightarrow E_1 \qquad E + E_1 \vdash dec_2 \Rightarrow E_2}{E \vdash dec_1\ \langle\texttt{;}\rangle\ dec_2 \Rightarrow E_1 + E_2} \tag{123}$$

## Value Bindings $\boxed{E \vdash valbind \Rightarrow VE/p}$

$$\frac{E \vdash exp \Rightarrow v \qquad E, v \vdash pat \Rightarrow VE \qquad \langle E \vdash valbind \Rightarrow VE' \rangle}{E \vdash pat \texttt{ = } exp\ \langle\texttt{and}\ valbind\rangle \Rightarrow VE\ \langle +\ VE' \rangle} \tag{124}$$

$$\frac{E \vdash exp \Rightarrow v \qquad E, v \vdash pat \Rightarrow \text{FAIL}}{E \vdash pat \texttt{ = } exp\ \langle\texttt{and}\ valbind\rangle \Rightarrow [\text{Bind}]} \tag{125}$$

$$\frac{E \vdash valbind \Rightarrow VE}{E \vdash \texttt{rec}\ valbind \Rightarrow \text{Rec}\,VE} \tag{126}$$

## Type Bindings $\boxed{\vdash typbind \Rightarrow TE}$

$$\frac{\langle\vdash typbind \Rightarrow TE\rangle}{\vdash tyvarseq\ tycon \texttt{ = } ty\ \langle\texttt{and}\ typbind\rangle \Rightarrow \{tycon \mapsto \{\}\}\langle +TE\rangle} \tag{127}$$

## Datatype Bindings $\boxed{\vdash datbind \Rightarrow VE, TE}$

$$\frac{\vdash conbind \Rightarrow VE \qquad \langle\vdash datbind' \Rightarrow VE', TE'\rangle}{\vdash tyvarseq\ tycon \texttt{=} conbind\ \langle\texttt{and}\ datbind'\rangle \Rightarrow VE\langle +VE'\rangle, \{tycon \mapsto VE\}\langle +TE'\rangle} \tag{128}$$

## Constructor Bindings

$$\boxed{\vdash \textit{conbind} \Rightarrow VE}$$

$$\frac{\langle \vdash \textit{conbind} \Rightarrow VE \rangle}{\vdash \textit{vid} \langle \mid \textit{conbind} \rangle \Rightarrow \{\textit{vid} \mapsto (\textit{vid}, c)\} \langle +VE \rangle} \tag{129}$$

## Exception Bindings

$$\boxed{E \vdash \textit{exbind} \Rightarrow VE}$$

$$\frac{\textit{en} \notin \textit{ens of } s \quad s' = s + \{\textit{en}\} \quad \langle s', E \vdash \textit{exbind} \Rightarrow VE, s'' \rangle}{s, E \vdash \textit{vid} \langle \text{and } \textit{exbind} \rangle \Rightarrow \{\textit{vid} \mapsto (\textit{en}, \mathsf{e})\} \langle + VE \rangle, \ s' \langle' \rangle} \tag{130}$$

$$\frac{E(\textit{longvid}) = (\textit{en}, \mathsf{e}) \quad \langle E \vdash \textit{exbind} \Rightarrow VE \rangle}{E \vdash \textit{vid} = \textit{longvid} \langle \text{and } \textit{exbind} \rangle \Rightarrow \{\textit{vid} \mapsto (\textit{en}, \mathsf{e})\} \langle + VE \rangle} \tag{131}$$

*Comments:*

(130) The two side conditions ensure that a new exception name is generated and recorded as "used" in subsequent states.

## Atomic Patterns

$$\boxed{E, v \vdash \textit{atpat} \Rightarrow VE/\text{FAIL}}$$

$$\frac{}{E, v \vdash \_ \Rightarrow \{\}} \tag{132}$$

$$\frac{v = \text{val}(\textit{scon})}{E, v \vdash \textit{scon} \Rightarrow \{\}} \tag{133}$$

$$\frac{v \neq \text{val}(\textit{scon})}{E, v \vdash \textit{scon} \Rightarrow \text{FAIL}} \tag{134}$$

$$\frac{\textit{vid} \notin \text{Dom}(E) \text{ or } \textit{is of } E(\textit{vid}) = \mathsf{v}}{E, v \vdash \textit{vid} \Rightarrow \{\textit{vid} \mapsto (v, \mathsf{v})\}} \tag{135}$$

$$\frac{E(\textit{longvid}) = (v, \textit{is}) \quad \textit{is} \neq \mathsf{v}}{E, v \vdash \textit{longvid} \Rightarrow \{\}} \tag{136}$$

$$\frac{E(\textit{longvid}) = (v', \textit{is}) \quad \textit{is} \neq \mathsf{v} \quad v \neq v'}{E, v \vdash \textit{longvid} \Rightarrow \text{FAIL}} \tag{137}$$

$$\frac{v = \{\} \langle +r \rangle \text{ in Val} \quad \langle E, r \vdash \textit{patrow} \Rightarrow VE/\text{FAIL} \rangle}{E, v \vdash \{ \langle \textit{patrow} \rangle \} \Rightarrow \{\} \langle +VE/\text{FAIL} \rangle} \tag{138}$$

$$\frac{E, v \vdash \textit{pat} \Rightarrow VE/\text{FAIL}}{E, v \vdash ( \textit{pat} ) \Rightarrow VE/\text{FAIL}} \tag{139}$$

*Comments:*

(134), (137) Any evaluation resulting in FAIL must do so because rule 134, rule 137, rule 145, or rule 147 has been applied.

**Pattern Rows**                         $\boxed{E, r \vdash patrow \Rightarrow VE/\text{FAIL}}$

$$\frac{}{E, r \vdash \ldots \Rightarrow \{\}} \tag{140}$$

$$\frac{E, r(lab) \vdash pat \Rightarrow \text{FAIL}}{E, r \vdash lab = pat \,\langle\, , \, patrow\rangle \Rightarrow \text{FAIL}} \tag{141}$$

$$\frac{E, r(lab) \vdash pat \Rightarrow VE \qquad \langle E, r \vdash patrow \Rightarrow VE'/\text{FAIL}\rangle}{E, r \vdash lab = pat \,\langle\, , \, patrow\rangle \Rightarrow VE\langle + \, VE'/\text{FAIL}\rangle} \tag{142}$$

*Comments:*

(141),(142) For well-typed programs *lab* will be in the domain of $r$.

**Patterns**                             $\boxed{E, v \vdash pat \Rightarrow VE/\text{FAIL}}$

$$\frac{E, v \vdash atpat \Rightarrow VE/\text{FAIL}}{E, v \vdash atpat \Rightarrow VE/\text{FAIL}} \tag{143}$$

$$\frac{\begin{array}{ccc} E(longvid) = (vid, \text{c}) & vid \neq \texttt{ref} & v = (vid, v') \\ & E, v' \vdash atpat \Rightarrow VE/\text{FAIL} & \end{array}}{E, v \vdash longvid \; atpat \Rightarrow VE/\text{FAIL}} \tag{144}$$

$$\frac{E(longvid) = (vid, \text{c}) \qquad vid \neq \texttt{ref} \qquad v \notin \{vid\} \times \text{Val}}{E, v \vdash longvid \; atpat \Rightarrow \text{FAIL}} \tag{145}$$

$$\frac{\begin{array}{cc} E(longvid) = (en, \text{e}) & v = (en, v') \\ E, v' \vdash atpat \Rightarrow VE/\text{FAIL} & \end{array}}{E, v \vdash longvid \; atpat \Rightarrow VE/\text{FAIL}} \tag{146}$$

$$\frac{E(longvid) = (en, \text{e}) \qquad v \notin \{en\} \times \text{Val}}{E, v \vdash longvid \; atpat \Rightarrow \text{FAIL}} \tag{147}$$

$$\frac{s(a) = v \qquad s, E, v \vdash atpat \Rightarrow VE/\text{FAIL}, s}{s, E, a \vdash \texttt{ref} \; atpat \Rightarrow VE/\text{FAIL}, s} \tag{148}$$

$$\frac{E, v \vdash pat \Rightarrow VE/\text{FAIL}}{E, v \vdash vid \; \texttt{as} \; pat \Rightarrow \{vid \mapsto (v, \text{v})\} + VE/\text{FAIL}} \tag{149}$$

*Comments:*

(145),(147) Any evaluation resulting in FAIL must do so because rule 134,  rule 137, rule 145, or rule 147 has been applied.

# 7 Dynamic Semantics for Modules

## 7.1 Reduced Syntax

Since signature expressions are mostly dealt with in the static semantics, the dynamic semantics need only take limited account of them. However, they cannot be ignored completely; the reason is that an explicit signature ascription plays the rôle of restricting the "view" of a structure – that is, restricting the domains of its component environments and imposing identifier status on value identifiers. The syntax is therefore reduced by the following transformations (in addition to those for the Core), for the purpose of the dynamic semantics of Modules:

- Qualifications "of *ty*" are omitted from constructor and exception descriptions.

- Any qualification **sharing type** $\cdots$ on a specification or **where type** $\cdots$ on a signature expression is omitted.

## 7.2 Compound Objects

The compound objects for the Modules dynamic semantics, extra to those for the Core dynamic semantics, are shown in Figure 14. An *interface* $I \in$ Int represents a "view" of a

$$
\begin{array}{rcl}
(strid : I, strexp, B) & \in & \text{FunctorClosure} \\
& & = (\text{StrId} \times \text{Int}) \times \text{StrExp} \times \text{Basis} \\
I \text{ or } (SI, TI, VI) & \in & \text{Int} = \text{StrInt} \times \text{TyInt} \times \text{ValInt} \\
SI & \in & \text{StrInt} = \text{StrId} \xrightarrow{\text{fin}} \text{Int} \\
TI & \in & \text{TyInt} = \text{TyCon} \xrightarrow{\text{fin}} \text{ValInt} \\
VI & \in & \text{ValInt} = \text{VId} \xrightarrow{\text{fin}} \text{IdStatus} \\
G & \in & \text{SigEnv} = \text{SigId} \xrightarrow{\text{fin}} \text{Int} \\
F & \in & \text{FunEnv} = \text{FunId} \xrightarrow{\text{fin}} \text{FunctorClosure} \\
(F, G, E) \text{ or } B & \in & \text{Basis} = \text{FunEnv} \times \text{SigEnv} \times \text{Env} \\
(G, I) \text{ or } IB & \in & \text{IntBasis} = \text{SigEnv} \times \text{Int}
\end{array}
$$

Figure 14: Compound Semantic Objects

structure. Specifications and signature expressions will evaluate to interfaces; moreover, during the evaluation of a specification or signature expression, structures (to which a specification or signature expression may refer via datatype replicating specifications) are represented only by their interfaces. To extract a value interface from a dynamic value environment we define the operation Inter : ValEnv $\to$ ValInt as follows:

$$
\text{Inter}(VE) = \{vid \mapsto is \; ; \; VE(vid) = (v, is)\}
$$

In other words, Inter($VE$) is the value interface obtained from $VE$ by removing all values from $VE$. We then extend Inter to a function Inter : Env $\rightarrow$ Int as follows:

$$\text{Inter}(SE, TE, VE) \;=\; (SI, TI, VI)$$

where $VI = \text{Inter}(VE)$ and

$$SI \;=\; \{strid \mapsto \text{Inter}\, E \; ; \; SE(strid) = E\}$$
$$TI \;=\; \{tycon \mapsto \text{Inter}\, VE' \; ; \; TE(tycon) = VE'\}$$

An *interface basis* $IB = (G, I)$ is a value-free part of a basis, sufficient to evaluate signature expressions and specifications. The function Inter is extended to create an interface basis from a basis $B$ as follows:

$$\text{Inter}(F, G, E) \;=\; (G, \text{Inter}\, E)$$

A further operation
$$\downarrow : \; \text{Env} \times \text{Int} \rightarrow \text{Env}$$
is required, to cut down an environment $E$ to a given interface $I$, representing the effect of an explicit signature ascription. We first define $\downarrow$: ValEnv $\times$ ValInt $\rightarrow$ ValEnv by

$$VE \downarrow VI = \{vid \mapsto (v, is) \; ; \; VE(vid) = (v, is') \text{ and } VI(vid) = is\}$$

(Note that $VE$ and $VI$ need not have the same domain and that the identifier status is taken from $VI$.) We then define $\downarrow$: StrEnv $\times$ StrInt $\rightarrow$ StrEnv, $\downarrow$: TyEnv $\times$ TyInt $\rightarrow$ TyEnv and $\downarrow$: Env $\times$ Int $\rightarrow$ Env simultaneously as follows:

$$SE \downarrow SI = \{strid \mapsto E \downarrow I \; ; \; SE(strid) = E \text{ and } SI(strid) = I\}$$
$$TE \downarrow TI = \{tycon \mapsto VE' \downarrow VI' \; ; \; TE(tycon) = VE' \text{ and } TI(tycon) = VI'\}$$
$$(SE, TE, VE) \downarrow (SI, TI, VI) = (SE \downarrow SI, TE \downarrow TI, VE \downarrow VI)$$

It is important to note that an interface can also be obtained from the *static* value $\Sigma$ of a signature expression; it is obtained by first replacing every type structure $(\theta, VE)$ in the range of every type environment $TE$ by $VE$ and then replacing each pair $(\sigma, is)$ in the range of every value environment $VE$ by $is$. Thus in an implementation interfaces would naturally be obtained from the static elaboration; we choose to give separate rules here for obtaining them in the dynamic semantics since we wish to maintain our separation of the static and dynamic semantics, for reasons of presentation.

## 7.3   Inference Rules

The semantic rules allow sentences of the form

$$s, A \vdash phrase \Rightarrow A', s'$$

to be inferred, where $A$ is either a basis, a signature environment or empty, $A'$ is some semantic object and $s,s'$ are the states before and after the evaluation represented by the sentence. Some hypotheses in rules are not of this form; they are called *side-conditions*. The convention for options is the same as for the Core static semantics.

The state and exception conventions are adopted as in the Core dynamic semantics. However, it may be shown that the only Modules phrases whose evaluation may cause a side-effect or generate an exception packet are of the form *strexp*, *strdec*, *strbind* or *topdec*.

## Structure Expressions

$$\boxed{B \vdash strexp \Rightarrow E/p}$$

$$\frac{B \vdash strdec \Rightarrow E}{B \vdash \texttt{struct } strdec \texttt{ end} \Rightarrow E} \tag{150}$$

$$\frac{B(longstrid) = E}{B \vdash longstrid \Rightarrow E} \tag{151}$$

$$\frac{B \vdash strexp \Rightarrow E \qquad \text{Inter } B \vdash sigexp \Rightarrow I}{B \vdash strexp : sigexp \Rightarrow E \downarrow I} \tag{152}$$

$$\frac{B \vdash strexp \Rightarrow E \qquad \text{Inter } B \vdash sigexp \Rightarrow I}{B \vdash strexp \texttt{:>} sigexp \Rightarrow E \downarrow I} \tag{153}$$

$$\frac{B(funid) = (strid : I, strexp', B') \qquad B \vdash strexp \Rightarrow E \qquad B' + \{strid \mapsto E \downarrow I\} \vdash strexp' \Rightarrow E'}{B \vdash funid \ (\ strexp \ ) \ \Rightarrow E'} \tag{154}$$

$$\frac{B \vdash strdec \Rightarrow E \qquad B + E \vdash strexp \Rightarrow E'}{B \vdash \texttt{let } strdec \texttt{ in } strexp \texttt{ end} \Rightarrow E'} \tag{155}$$

*Comments:*

(154) Before the evaluation of the functor body *strexp'*, the actual argument $E$ is cut down by the formal parameter interface $I$, so that any opening of *strid* resulting from the evaluation of *strexp'* will produce no more components than anticipated during the static elaboration.

## Structure-level Declarations

$$\boxed{B \vdash strdec \Rightarrow E/p}$$

$$\frac{E \text{ of } B \vdash dec \Rightarrow E'}{B \vdash dec \Rightarrow E'} \tag{156}$$

$$\frac{B \vdash strbind \Rightarrow SE}{B \vdash \texttt{structure } strbind \Rightarrow SE \text{ in Env}} \tag{157}$$

$$\frac{B \vdash strdec_1 \Rightarrow E_1 \qquad B + E_1 \vdash strdec_2 \Rightarrow E_2}{B \vdash \texttt{local}\ strdec_1\ \texttt{in}\ strdec_2\ \texttt{end} \Rightarrow E_2} \qquad (158)$$

$$\frac{}{B \vdash \qquad \Rightarrow \{\}\ \text{in Env}} \qquad (159)$$

$$\frac{B \vdash strdec_1 \Rightarrow E_1 \qquad B + E_1 \vdash strdec_2 \Rightarrow E_2}{B \vdash strdec_1\ \langle;\rangle\ strdec_2 \Rightarrow E_1 + E_2} \qquad (160)$$

## Structure Bindings $\qquad\boxed{B \vdash strbind \Rightarrow SE/p}$

$$\frac{B \vdash strexp \Rightarrow E \qquad \langle B \vdash strbind \Rightarrow SE\rangle}{B \vdash strid\ \texttt{=}\ strexp\ \langle\texttt{and}\ strbind\rangle \Rightarrow \{strid \mapsto E\}\ \langle+\ SE\rangle} \qquad (161)$$

## Signature Expressions $\qquad\boxed{IB \vdash sigexp \Rightarrow I}$

$$\frac{IB \vdash spec \Rightarrow I}{IB \vdash \texttt{sig}\ spec\ \texttt{end} \Rightarrow I} \qquad (162)$$

$$\frac{IB(sigid) = I}{IB \vdash sigid \Rightarrow I} \qquad (163)$$

## Signature Declarations $\qquad\boxed{IB \vdash sigdec \Rightarrow G}$

$$\frac{IB \vdash sigbind \Rightarrow G}{IB \vdash \texttt{signature}\ sigbind \Rightarrow G} \qquad (164)$$

## Signature Bindings $\qquad\boxed{IB \vdash sigbind \Rightarrow G}$

$$\frac{IB \vdash sigexp \Rightarrow I \qquad \langle IB \vdash sigbind \Rightarrow G\rangle}{IB \vdash sigid\ \texttt{=}\ sigexp\ \langle\texttt{and}\ sigbind\rangle \Rightarrow \{sigid \mapsto I\}\ \langle+\ G\rangle} \qquad (165)$$

## Specifications $\qquad\boxed{IB \vdash spec \Rightarrow I}$

$$\frac{\vdash valdesc \Rightarrow VI}{IB \vdash \texttt{val}\ valdesc \Rightarrow VI\ \text{in Int}} \qquad (166)$$

$$\frac{\vdash typdesc \Rightarrow TI}{IB \vdash \texttt{type}\ typdesc \Rightarrow TI\ \text{in Int}} \qquad (167)$$

$$\frac{\vdash typdesc \Rightarrow TI}{IB \vdash \texttt{eqtype}\ typdesc \Rightarrow TI\ \text{in Int}} \qquad (168)$$

$$\frac{\vdash datdesc \Rightarrow VI, TI}{IB \vdash \texttt{datatype}\ datdesc \Rightarrow (VI, TI)\ \text{in Int}} \qquad (169)$$

$$\frac{IB(longtycon) = VI \qquad TI = \{tycon \mapsto VI\}}{IB \vdash \texttt{datatype}\ tycon = \texttt{datatype}\ longtycon \Rightarrow (VI, TI)\ \text{in Int}} \qquad (170)$$

$$\frac{\vdash exdesc \Rightarrow VI}{IB \vdash \texttt{exception}\ exdesc \Rightarrow VI\ \text{in Int}} \qquad (171)$$

$$\frac{IB \vdash strdesc \Rightarrow SI}{IB \vdash \texttt{structure}\ strdesc \Rightarrow SI\ \text{in Int}} \qquad (172)$$

$$\frac{IB \vdash sigexp \Rightarrow I}{IB \vdash \texttt{include}\ sigexp \Rightarrow I} \qquad (173)$$

$$\frac{}{IB \vdash \qquad \Rightarrow \{\}\ \text{in Int}} \qquad (174)$$

$$\frac{IB \vdash spec_1 \Rightarrow I_1 \qquad IB + I_1 \vdash spec_2 \Rightarrow I_2}{IB \vdash spec_1\ \langle\texttt{;}\rangle\ spec_2 \Rightarrow I_1 + I_2} \qquad (175)$$

## Value Descriptions                    $\boxed{\vdash valdesc \Rightarrow VI}$

$$\frac{\langle\vdash valdesc \Rightarrow VI\rangle}{\vdash vid\ \langle\texttt{and}\ valdesc\rangle \Rightarrow \{vid \mapsto \texttt{v}\}\ \langle+VI\rangle} \qquad (176)$$

## Type Descriptions                     $\boxed{\vdash typdesc \Rightarrow TI}$

$$\frac{\langle\vdash typdesc \Rightarrow TI\rangle}{\vdash tyvarseq\ tycon\ \langle\texttt{and}\ typdesc\rangle \Rightarrow \{tycon \mapsto \{\}\}\langle+TI\rangle} \qquad (177)$$

## Datatype Descriptions                 $\boxed{\vdash datdesc \Rightarrow VI, TI}$

$$\frac{\vdash condesc \Rightarrow VI \qquad \langle\vdash datdesc' \Rightarrow VI', TI'\rangle}{\vdash tyvarseq\ tycon = condesc\ \langle\texttt{and}\ datdesc'\rangle \Rightarrow VI\ \langle+VI'\rangle, \{tycon \mapsto VI\}\langle+TI'\rangle} \qquad (178)$$

## Constructor Descriptions

$$\boxed{\vdash condesc \Rightarrow VI}$$

$$\frac{\langle\vdash condesc \Rightarrow VI\rangle}{\vdash vid\ \langle\ |\ condesc\rangle \Rightarrow \{vid \mapsto \mathsf{c}\}\ \langle + VI\rangle} \tag{179}$$

## Exception Descriptions

$$\boxed{\vdash exdesc \Rightarrow VI}$$

$$\frac{\langle\vdash exdesc \Rightarrow VI\rangle}{\vdash vid\ \langle\mathsf{and}\ exdesc\rangle \Rightarrow \{vid \mapsto \mathsf{e}\}\ \langle + VI\rangle} \tag{180}$$

## Structure Descriptions

$$\boxed{IB \vdash strdesc \Rightarrow SI}$$

$$\frac{IB \vdash sigexp \Rightarrow I \quad \langle IB \vdash strdesc \Rightarrow SI\rangle}{IB \vdash strid : sigexp\ \langle\mathsf{and}\ strdesc\rangle \Rightarrow \{strid \mapsto I\}\ \langle + SI\rangle} \tag{181}$$

## Functor Bindings

$$\boxed{B \vdash funbind \Rightarrow F}$$

$$\frac{\mathrm{Inter}\ B \vdash sigexp \Rightarrow I \quad \langle IB \vdash funbind \Rightarrow F\rangle}{\begin{array}{c} IB \vdash funid\ (\ strid : sigexp\ )\ =\ strexp\ \langle\mathsf{and}\ funbind\rangle \Rightarrow \\ \{funid \mapsto (strid : I, strexp, B)\}\ \langle + F\rangle \end{array}} \tag{182}$$

## Functor Declarations

$$\boxed{B \vdash fundec \Rightarrow F}$$

$$\frac{B \vdash funbind \Rightarrow F}{B \vdash \mathsf{functor}\ funbind \Rightarrow F} \tag{183}$$

## Top-level Declarations

$$\boxed{B \vdash topdec \Rightarrow B'/p}$$

$$\frac{B \vdash strdec \Rightarrow E \quad B' = E\ \mathrm{in\ Basis} \quad \langle B + B' \vdash topdec \Rightarrow B''\rangle}{B \vdash strdec\ \langle topdec\rangle \Rightarrow B'\langle'\rangle} \tag{184}$$

$$\frac{\mathrm{Inter}\ B \vdash sigdec \Rightarrow G \quad B' = G\ \mathrm{in\ Basis} \quad \langle B + B' \vdash topdec \Rightarrow B''\rangle}{B \vdash sigdec\ \langle topdec\rangle \Rightarrow B'\langle'\rangle} \tag{185}$$

$$\frac{B \vdash fundec \Rightarrow F \quad B' = F\ \mathrm{in\ Basis} \quad \langle B + B' \vdash topdec \Rightarrow B''\rangle}{B \vdash fundec\ \langle topdec\rangle \Rightarrow B'\langle'\rangle} \tag{186}$$

# 8 Programs

The phrase class Program of programs is defined as follows

$$program ::= topdec \; ; \; \langle program \rangle$$

Hitherto, the semantic rules have not exposed the interactive nature of the language. During an ML session the user can type in a phrase, more precisely a phrase of the form *topdec* as defined in Figure 8, page 14. Upon the following semicolon, the machine will then attempt to parse, elaborate and evaluate the phrase returning either a result or, if any of the phases fail, an error message. The outcome is significant for what the user subsequently types, so we need to answer questions such as: if the elaboration of a top-level declaration succeeds, but its evaluation fails, then does the result of the elaboration get recorded in the static basis?

In practice, ML implementations may provide a directive as a form of top-level declaration for including programs from files rather than directly from the terminal. In case a file consists of a sequence of top-level declarations (separated by semicolons) and the machine detects an error in one of these, it is probably sensible to abort the execution of the directive. Rather than introducing a distinction between, say, batch programs and interactive programs, we shall tacitly regard all programs as interactive, and leave to implementers to clarify how the inclusion of files, if provided, affects the updating of the static and dynamic basis. Moreover, we shall focus on elaboration and evaluation and leave the handling of parse errors to implementers (since it naturally depends on the kind of parser being employed). Hence, in this section the *execution* of a program means the combined elaboration and evaluation of the program.

So far, for simplicity, we have used the same notation $B$ to stand for both a static and a dynamic basis, and this has been possible because we have never needed to discuss static and dynamic semantics at the same time. In giving the semantics of programs, however, let us rename as StaticBasis the class Basis defined in the static semantics of modules, Section 5.1, and let us use $B_{STAT}$ to range over StaticBasis. Similarly, let us rename as DynamicBasis the class Basis defined in the dynamic semantics of modules, Section 7.2, and let us use $B_{DYN}$ to range over DynamicBasis. We now define

$$B \text{ or } (B_{STAT}, B_{DYN}) \in \text{Basis} = \text{StaticBasis} \times \text{DynamicBasis}.$$

Further, we shall use $\vdash_{STAT}$ for elaboration as defined in Section 5, and $\vdash_{DYN}$ for evaluation as defined in Section 7. Then $\vdash$ will be reserved for the execution of programs, which thus is expressed by a sentence of the form

$$s, B \vdash program \Rightarrow B', s'$$

This may be read as follows: starting in basis $B$ with state $s$ the execution of *program* results in a basis $B'$ and a state $s'$.

It must be understood that executing a program never results in an exception. If the evaluation of a *topdec* yields an exception (for instance because of a **raise** expression)

then the result of executing the program "*topdec* ;" is the original basis together with
the state which is in force when the exception is generated. In particular, the exception
convention of Section 6.7 is not applicable to the ensuing rules.

We represent the non-elaboration of a top-level declaration by $\dots \vdash_{\text{STAT}} topdec \not\Rightarrow$.

## Programs
$$\boxed{s, B \vdash program \Rightarrow B', s'}$$

$$\frac{B_{\text{STAT}} \text{ of } B \vdash_{\text{STAT}} topdec \not\Rightarrow \qquad \langle s, B \vdash program \Rightarrow B', s' \rangle}{s, B \vdash topdec \ ; \ \langle program \rangle \Rightarrow B\langle' \rangle, s\langle' \rangle} \tag{187}$$

$$\frac{\begin{array}{c} B_{\text{STAT}} \text{ of } B \vdash_{\text{STAT}} topdec \Rightarrow B_{\text{STAT}}^{(1)} \\ s, B_{\text{DYN}} \text{ of } B \vdash_{\text{DYN}} topdec \Rightarrow p, s' \qquad \langle s', B \vdash program \Rightarrow B', s'' \rangle \end{array}}{s, B \vdash topdec \ ; \ \langle program \rangle \Rightarrow B\langle' \rangle, s'\langle' \rangle} \tag{188}$$

$$\frac{\begin{array}{c} B_{\text{STAT}} \text{ of } B \vdash_{\text{STAT}} topdec \Rightarrow B_{\text{STAT}}^{(1)} \\ s, B_{\text{DYN}} \text{ of } B \vdash_{\text{DYN}} topdec \Rightarrow B_{\text{DYN}}^{(1)}, s' \quad B' = B \oplus (B_{\text{STAT}}^{(1)}, B_{\text{DYN}}^{(1)}) \\ \langle s', B' \vdash program \Rightarrow B'', s'' \rangle \end{array}}{s, B \vdash topdec \ ; \ \langle program \rangle \Rightarrow B'\langle' \rangle, s'\langle' \rangle} \tag{189}$$

*Comments:*

(187) A failing elaboration has no effect whatever.

(188) An evaluation which yields an exception nullifies the change in the static basis,
but does not nullify side-effects on the state which may have occurred before the
exception was raised.

## Core language Programs

A program is called a *core language program* if it can be parsed in the reduced grammar
defined as follows:

1. Replace the definition of top-level declarations by

$$topdec \ ::= \ strdec$$

2. Replace the definition of structure-level declarations by

$$strdec \ ::= \ dec$$

# A  Appendix: Derived Forms

Several derived grammatical forms are provided in the Core; they are presented in Figures 15, 16 and 17. Each derived form is given with its equivalent form. Thus, each row of the tables should be considered as a rewriting rule

$$\text{Derived form} \implies \text{Equivalent form}$$

and these rules may be applied repeatedly to a phrase until it is transformed into a phrase of the bare language. See Appendix B for the full Core grammar, including all the derived forms.

In the derived forms for tuples, in terms of records, we use $\overline{n}$ to mean the ML numeral which stands for the natural number $n$.

Note that a new phrase class  FvalBind  of function-value bindings is introduced, accompanied by a new declaration form  fun *tyvarseq fvalbind* . The mixed forms  val *tyvarseq* rec *fvalbind* ,  val *tyvarseq fvalbind*  and  fun *tyvarseq valbind*  are not allowed – though the first form arises during translation into the bare language.

The following notes refer to Figure 17:

- There is a version of the derived form for function-value binding which allows the function identifier to be infixed; see Figure 21 in Appendix B.

- In the two forms involving  withtype , the identifiers bound by  *datbind*  and by *typbind* must be distinct. Then the transformed binding  *datbind'*  in the equivalent form is obtained from  *datbind*  by expanding out all the definitions made by  *typbind*. More precisely, if  *typbind*  is

$$tyvarseq_1 \; tycon_1 = ty_1 \; \text{and} \; \cdots \; \text{and} \; tyvarseq_n \; tycon_n = ty_n$$

then *datbind'* is the result of simultaneous replacement (in  *datbind*) of every type expression  $tyseq_i \; tycon_i \;\; (1 \le i \le n)$  by the corresponding defining expression

$$ty_i \{ tyseq_i / tyvarseq_i \}$$

Figure 18 shows derived forms for functors. They allow functors to take, say, a single type or value as a parameter, in cases where it would seem clumsy to "wrap up" the argument as a structure expression.

Finally, Figure 19 shows the derived forms for specifications and signature expressions. The last derived form for specifications allows sharing between structure identifiers as a shorthand for type sharing specifications. The phrase

$$spec \; \textsf{sharing} \; longstrid_1 = \cdots = longstrid_k$$

is a derived form whose equivalent form is

Derived Form                                Equivalent Form

**Expressions** *exp*

| Derived Form | Equivalent Form | |
|---|---|---|
| () | { } | |
| $(exp_1, \cdots, exp_n)$ | $\{1=exp_1, \cdots, \overline{n}=exp_n\}$ | $(n \geq 2)$ |
| # *lab* | fn $\{lab=vid, \ldots\}$ => *vid* | (*vid* new) |
| case *exp* of *match* | (fn *match*)(*exp*) | |
| if $exp_1$ then $exp_2$ else $exp_3$ | case $exp_1$ of true => $exp_2$ <br> &#124; false => $exp_3$ | |
| $exp_1$ orelse $exp_2$ | if $exp_1$ then true else $exp_2$ | |
| $exp_1$ andalso $exp_2$ | if $exp_1$ then $exp_2$ else false | |
| $(exp_1 ; \cdots ; exp_n ; exp)$ | case $exp_1$ of (_) => <br> $\cdots$ <br> case $exp_n$ of (_) => *exp* | $(n \geq 1)$ |
| let *dec* in <br>   $exp_1 ; \cdots ; exp_n$ end | let *dec* in <br>   $(exp_1 ; \cdots ; exp_n)$ end | $(n \geq 2)$ |
| while $exp_1$ do $exp_2$ | let val rec *vid* = fn () => <br>   if $exp_1$ then $(exp_2; vid())$ else () <br> in *vid*() end | (*vid* new) |
| $[exp_1, \cdots, exp_n]$ | $exp_1 :: \cdots :: exp_n ::$ nil | $(n \geq 0)$ |

Figure 15: Derived forms of Expressions

   *spec*
     sharing type $longtycon_1$ = $longtycon'_1$
     $\cdots$
     sharing type $longtycon_m$ = $longtycon'_m$

determined as follows. First, note that *spec* specifies a set of (possibly long) type constructors and structure identifiers, either directly or via signature identifiers and include specifications. Then the equivalent form contains all type-sharing constraints of the form

    sharing type $longstrid_i.longtycon$ = $longstrid_j.longtycon$

$(1 \leq i < j \leq k)$, such that both sides of the equation are long type constructors specified by *spec*.

The meaning of the derived form does not depend on the order of the type-sharing constraints in the equivalent form.

| Derived Form | Equivalent Form | |
|---|---|---|
| **Patterns** *pat* | | |
| () | { } | |
| $(pat_1 , \cdots , pat_n)$ | $\{1{=}pat_1 , \cdots , \overline{n}{=}pat_n\}$ | $(n \geq 2)$ |
| $[pat_1 , \cdots , pat_n]$ | $pat_1 \;::\; \cdots \;::\; pat_n \;::\;$ `nil` | $(n \geq 0)$ |

| **Pattern Rows** *patrow* | |
|---|---|
| $vid\langle : ty\rangle \; \langle$as $pat\rangle \; \langle, \; patrow\rangle$ | $vid \;=\; vid\langle : ty\rangle \; \langle$as $pat\rangle \; \langle, \; patrow\rangle$ |

| **Type Expressions** *ty* | | |
|---|---|---|
| $ty_1 * \cdots * ty_n$ | $\{1{:}ty_1 , \cdots , \overline{n}{:}ty_n\}$ | $(n \geq 2)$ |

Figure 16: Derived forms of Patterns and Type Expressions

| Derived Form | Equivalent Form |
|---|---|
| **Function-value Bindings** *fvalbind* | |
| $\langle$op$\rangle vid \; atpat_{11}\cdots atpat_{1n}\langle : ty\rangle \;=\; exp_1$ <br> $\mid \langle$op$\rangle vid \; atpat_{21}\cdots atpat_{2n}\langle : ty\rangle \;=\; exp_2$ <br> $\mid \quad \cdots \qquad \cdots$ <br> $\mid \langle$op$\rangle vid \; atpat_{m1}\cdots atpat_{mn}\langle : ty\rangle \;=\; exp_m$ <br> $\langle$and *fvalbind*$\rangle$ | $\langle$op$\rangle vid =$ `fn` $vid_1$`=>` $\cdots$ `fn` $vid_n$`=>` <br> `case` $(vid_1 , \cdots , vid_n)$ `of` <br> $(atpat_{11},\cdots, atpat_{1n}$ `)=>`$exp_1\langle : ty\rangle$ <br> $\mid (atpat_{21},\cdots, atpat_{2n}$ `)=>`$exp_2\langle : ty\rangle$ <br> $\mid \quad \cdots \qquad \cdots$ <br> $\mid (atpat_{m1},\cdots, atpat_{mn}$ `)=>`$exp_m\langle : ty\rangle$ <br> $\langle$and *fvalbind*$\rangle$ |

$(m, n \geq 1; \; vid_1,\cdots, vid_n \text{ distinct and new})$

| **Declarations** *dec* | |
|---|---|
| `fun` *tyvarseq fvalbind* | `val` *tyvarseq* `rec` *fvalbind* |
| `datatype` *datbind* `withtype` *typbind* | `datatype` *datbind'* `;` `type` *typbind* |
| `abstype` *datbind* `withtype` *typbind* <br> `with` *dec* `end` | `abstype` *datbind'* <br> `with type` *typbind* `;` *dec* `end` |

(see note in text concerning *datbind'*)

Figure 17: Derived forms of Function-value Bindings and Declarations

|                      Derived Form                      |                      Equivalent Form                      |

**Structure Bindings** *strbind*

| Derived Form | Equivalent Form |
| --- | --- |
| *strid* : *sigexp*=*strexp* ⟨and *strbind*⟩ | *strid*=*strexp* : *sigexp* ⟨and *strbind*⟩ |
| *strid* :>*sigexp*=*strexp* ⟨and *strbind*⟩ | *strid*=*strexp* :>*sigexp* ⟨and *strbind*⟩ |

**Structure Expressions** *strexp*

| Derived Form | Equivalent Form |
| --- | --- |
| *funid* ( *strdec* ) | *funid* ( struct *strdec* end ) |

**Functor Bindings** *funbind*

| Derived Form | Equivalent Form |
| --- | --- |
| *funid* (*strid* : *sigexp*) : *sigexp′* = *strexp* ⟨and *funbind*⟩ | *funid* (*strid* : *sigexp*) = *strexp* : *sigexp′* ⟨and *funbind*⟩ |
| *funid* (*strid* : *sigexp*) :>*sigexp′* = *strexp* ⟨and *funbind*⟩ | *funid* (*strid* : *sigexp*) = *strexp* :>*sigexp′* ⟨and *funbind*⟩ |
| *funid* ( *spec* ) ⟨: *sigexp*⟩ = *strexp* ⟨and *funbind*⟩ | *funid* ( *strid*$_\nu$ : sig *spec* end ) = let open *strid*$_\nu$ in *strexp*⟨: *sigexp*⟩ end ⟨and *funbind*⟩ |
| *funid* ( *spec* ) ⟨:> *sigexp*⟩ = *strexp* ⟨and *funbind*⟩ | *funid* ( *strid*$_\nu$ : sig *spec* end ) = let open *strid*$_\nu$ in *strexp*⟨:>*sigexp*⟩ end ⟨and *funbind*⟩ |

$$(strid_\nu \text{ new})$$

**Programs** *program*

| Derived Form | Equivalent Form |
| --- | --- |
| *exp* ; ⟨*program*⟩ | val it = *exp* ; ⟨*program*⟩ |

Figure 18: Derived forms of Functors, Structure Bindings and Programs

| Derived Form | Equivalent Form |
|---|---|

**Specifications** *spec*

| | |
|---|---|
| **type** *tyvarseq tycon* = *ty* | **include**<br>**sig type** *tyvarseq tycon*<br>**end where type** *tyvarseq tycon* = *ty* |
| **type** $tyvarseq_1$ $tycon_1$ = $ty_1$<br>**and** $\cdots$<br>$\ldots$<br>**and** $tyvarseq_n$ $tycon_n$ = $ty_n$ | **type** $tyvarseq_1$ $tycon_1$ = $ty_1$<br>**type** $\cdots$<br>$\ldots$<br>**type** $tyvarseq_n$ $tycon_n$ = $ty_n$ |
| **include** $sigid_1 \cdots sigid_n$ | **include** $sigid_1; \cdots ;$ **include** $sigid_n$ |
| *spec* **sharing** $longstrid_1$ = $\cdots$<br>$\quad\quad\quad\quad$ = $longstrid_k$ | *spec*<br>**sharing type** $longtycon_1$ =<br>$\quad\quad\quad\quad longtycon_1'$<br>$\ldots$<br>**sharing type** $longtycon_m$ =<br>$\quad\quad\quad\quad longtycon_m'$ |

(see note in text concerning $longtycon_1, \ldots, longtycon_m'$)

**Signature Expressions** *sigexp*

| | |
|---|---|
| *sigexp*<br>**where type** $tyvarseq_1$ $longtycon_1$ = $ty_1$<br>**and type** $\cdots$<br>$\ldots$<br>**and type** $tyvarseq_n$ $longtycon_n$ = $ty_n$ | *sigexp*<br>**where type** $tyvarseq_1$ $longtycon_1$ = $ty_1$<br>**where type** $\cdots$<br>$\ldots$<br>**where type** $tyvarseq_n$ $longtycon_n$ = $ty_n$ |

Figure 19: Derived forms of Specifications and Signature Expressions

# B   Appendix: Full Grammar

The full grammar of programs is exactly as given at the start of Section 8.

The full grammar of Modules consists of the grammar of Figures 5–8 in Section 3, together with the derived forms of Figures 18 and 19 in Appendix A.

The remainder of this Appendix is devoted to the full grammar of the Core. Roughly, it consists of the grammar of Section 2 augmented by the derived forms of Appendix A. But there is a further difference: two additional subclasses of the phrase class Exp are introduced, namely AppExp (application expressions) and InfExp (infix expressions). The inclusion relation among the four classes is as follows:

$$\text{AtExp} \subset \text{AppExp} \subset \text{InfExp} \subset \text{Exp}$$

The effect is that certain phrases, such as "2 + while $\cdots$ do $\cdots$ ", are now disallowed.

The grammatical rules are displayed in Figures 20, 21, 22 and 23. The grammatical conventions are exactly as in Section 2, namely:

- The brackets $\langle\ \rangle$ enclose optional phrases.

- For any syntax class X (over which $x$ ranges) we define the syntax class Xseq (over which $xseq$ ranges) as follows:

  $$xseq \quad ::= \quad x \qquad\qquad \text{(singleton sequence)}$$
  $$\phantom{xseq \quad ::= \quad} \text{(empty sequence)}$$
  $$(x_1,\cdots,x_n) \quad \text{(sequence, } n \geq 1)$$

  (Note that the "$\cdots$" used here, a meta-symbol indicating syntactic repetition, must not be confused with "..." which is a reserved word of the language.)

- Alternative forms for each phrase class are in order of decreasing precedence. This precedence resolves ambiguity in parsing in the following way. Suppose that a phrase class — we take $exp$ as an example — has two alternative forms $F_1$ and $F_2$, such that $F_1$ ends with an $exp$ and $F_2$ starts with an $exp$. A specific case is

  $F_1$:   if $exp_1$ then $exp_2$ else $exp_3$
  $F_2$:   $exp$ handle $match$

It will be enough to see how ambiguity is resolved in this specific case.

Suppose that the lexical sequence

$$\cdots \cdots \text{ if } \cdots \text{ then } \cdots \text{ else } exp \text{ handle } \cdots \cdots$$

is to be parsed, where $exp$ stands for a lexical sequence which is already determined as a subphrase (if necessary by applying the precedence rule). Then the higher precedence of $F_2$ (in this case) dictates that *exp* associates to the right, i.e. that the correct parse takes the form

$$\cdots \cdots \texttt{if} \cdots \texttt{then} \cdots \texttt{else} \; (\textit{exp} \; \texttt{handle} \cdots) \cdots$$

not the form

$$\cdots (\cdots \texttt{if} \cdots \texttt{then} \cdots \texttt{else} \; \textit{exp}) \; \texttt{handle} \cdots \cdots$$

Note particularly that the use of precedence does not decrease the class of admissible phrases; it merely rejects alternative ways of parsing certain phrases. In particular, the purpose is not to prevent a phrase, which is an instance of a form with higher precedence, having a constituent which is an instance of a form with lower precedence. Thus for example

$$\texttt{if} \cdots \texttt{then while} \cdots \texttt{do} \cdots \texttt{else while} \cdots \texttt{do} \cdots$$

is quite admissible, and will be parsed as

$$\texttt{if} \cdots \texttt{then (while} \cdots \texttt{do} \cdots) \texttt{else (while} \cdots \texttt{do} \cdots)$$

- L (resp. R) means left (resp. right) association.

- The syntax of types binds more tightly than that of expressions.

- Each iterated construct (e.g. *match*, $\cdots$ ) extends as far right as possible; thus, parentheses may be needed around an expression which terminates with a match, e.g. "fn *match*", if this occurs within a larger match.

| *atexp* | ::= | *scon* | special constant |
| | | ⟨op⟩*longvid* | value identifier |
| | | { ⟨*exprow*⟩ } | record |
| | | # *lab* | record selector |
| | | () | 0-tuple |
| | | ($exp_1$ , $\cdots$ , $exp_n$) | $n$-tuple, $n \geq 2$ |
| | | [$exp_1$ , $\cdots$ , $exp_n$] | list, $n \geq 0$ |
| | | ($exp_1$ ; $\cdots$ ; $exp_n$) | sequence, $n \geq 2$ |
| | | let *dec* in $exp_1$ ; $\cdots$ ; $exp_n$ end | local declaration, $n \geq 1$ |
| | | ( *exp* ) | |
| *exprow* | ::= | *lab* = *exp* ⟨ , *exprow*⟩ | expression row |
| *appexp* | ::= | *atexp* | |
| | | *appexp atexp* | application expression |
| *infexp* | ::= | *appexp* | |
| | | $infexp_1$ *vid* $infexp_2$ | infix expression |
| *exp* | ::= | *infexp* | |
| | | *exp* : *ty* | typed (L) |
| | | $exp_1$ andalso $exp_2$ | conjunction |
| | | $exp_1$ orelse $exp_2$ | disjunction |
| | | *exp* handle *match* | handle exception |
| | | raise *exp* | raise exception |
| | | if $exp_1$ then $exp_2$ else $exp_3$ | conditional |
| | | while $exp_1$ do $exp_2$ | iteration |
| | | case *exp* of *match* | case analysis |
| | | fn *match* | function |
| *match* | ::= | *mrule* ⟨ | *match*⟩ | |
| *mrule* | ::= | *pat* => *exp* | |

Figure 20: Grammar: Expressions and Matches

| | | | |
|---|---|---|---|
| *dec* | ::= | `val` *tyvarseq valbind* | value declaration |
| | | `fun` *tyvarseq fvalbind* | function declaration |
| | | `type` *typbind* | type declaration |
| | | `datatype` *datbind* ⟨`withtype` *typbind*⟩ | datatype declaration |
| | | `datatype` *tycon* `= datatype` *longtycon* | datatype replication |
| | | `abstype` *datbind* ⟨`withtype` *typbind*⟩ | abstype declaration |
| | |    `with` *dec* `end` | |
| | | `exception` *exbind* | exception declaration |
| | | `local` *dec₁* `in` *dec₂* `end` | local declaration |
| | | `open` *longstrid₁* ⋯ *longstrid_n* | open declaration, $n \geq 1$ |
| | | | empty declaration |
| | | *dec₁* ⟨`;`⟩ *dec₂* | sequential declaration |
| | | `infix` ⟨*d*⟩ *vid₁* ⋯ *vid_n* | infix (L) directive, $n \geq 1$ |
| | | `infixr` ⟨*d*⟩ *vid₁* ⋯ *vid_n* | infix (R) directive, $n \geq 1$ |
| | | `nonfix` *vid₁* ⋯ *vid_n* | nonfix directive, $n \geq 1$ |
| | | | |
| *valbind* | ::= | *pat* `=` *exp* ⟨`and` *valbind*⟩ | |
| | | `rec` *valbind* | |
| | | | |
| *fvalbind* | ::= | ⟨`op`⟩*vid* *atpat₁₁*⋯*atpat₁ₙ*⟨`:` *ty*⟩`=`*exp₁* | $m, n \geq 1$ |
| | | `\|`⟨`op`⟩*vid*  *atpat₂₁*⋯*atpat₂ₙ*⟨`:` *ty*⟩`=`*exp₂* | See also note below |
| | | `\|`   ⋯    ⋯ | |
| | | `\|`⟨`op`⟩*vid*  *atpat_{m1}*⋯*atpat_{mn}*⟨`:` *ty*⟩`=`*exp_m* | |
| | |     ⟨`and` *fvalbind*⟩ | |
| | | | |
| *typbind* | ::= | *tyvarseq tycon* `=` *ty* ⟨`and` *typbind*⟩ | |
| | | | |
| *datbind* | ::= | *tyvarseq tycon* `=` *conbind* ⟨`and` *datbind*⟩ | |
| | | | |
| *conbind* | ::= | ⟨`op`⟩*vid* ⟨`of` *ty*⟩ ⟨ `\|` *conbind*⟩ | |
| | | | |
| *exbind* | ::= | ⟨`op`⟩*vid* ⟨`of` *ty*⟩ ⟨`and` *exbind*⟩ | |
| | | ⟨`op`⟩*vid* `=` ⟨`op`⟩*longvid* ⟨`and` *exbind*⟩ | |

Note: In the *fvalbind* form, if *vid* has infix status then either `op` must be present, or *vid* must be infixed. Thus, at the start of any clause, " `op` *vid* (*atpat*, *atpat′*) ⋯" may be written "(*atpat vid atpat′*) ⋯"; the parentheses may also be dropped if "`:` *ty*" or "`=`" follows immediately.

Figure 21: Grammar: Declarations and Bindings

| $atpat$ | $::=$ | _ | wildcard |
|---|---|---|---|
| | | $scon$ | special constant |
| | | $\langle\mathrm{op}\rangle longvid$ | value identifier |
| | | { $\langle patrow\rangle$ } | record |
| | | ( ) | 0-tuple |
| | | $(pat_1 , \cdots , pat_n)$ | $n$-tuple, $n \geq 2$ |
| | | $[pat_1 , \cdots , pat_n]$ | list, $n \geq 0$ |
| | | $( pat )$ | |
| $patrow$ | $::=$ | $\ldots$ | wildcard |
| | | $lab = pat \langle , patrow\rangle$ | pattern row |
| | | $vid\langle :ty\rangle \langle\mathrm{as}\ pat\rangle \langle , patrow\rangle$ | label as variable |
| $pat$ | $::=$ | $atpat$ | atomic |
| | | $\langle\mathrm{op}\rangle longvid\ atpat$ | constructed value |
| | | $pat_1\ vid\ pat_2$ | constructed value (infix) |
| | | $pat : ty$ | typed |
| | | $\langle\mathrm{op}\rangle vid\langle : ty\rangle \mathrm{as}\ pat$ | layered |

Figure 22: Grammar: Patterns

| $ty$ | $::=$ | $tyvar$ | type variable |
|---|---|---|---|
| | | { $\langle tyrow\rangle$ } | record type expression |
| | | $tyseq\ longtycon$ | type construction |
| | | $ty_1 * \cdots * ty_n$ | tuple type, $n \geq 2$ |
| | | $ty \rightarrow ty'$ | function type expression (R) |
| | | $( ty )$ | |
| $tyrow$ | $::=$ | $lab : ty \langle , tyrow\rangle$ | type-expression row |

Figure 23: Grammar: Type expressions

# C    Appendix: The Initial Static Basis

In this appendix (and the next) we define a minimal initial basis for execution. Richer bases may be provided by libraries. We shall indicate components of the initial basis by the subscript 0. The initial static basis is $B_0 = T_0, F_0, G_0, E_0$, where $F_0 = \{\}$, $G_0 = \{\}$ and

$$T_0 = \{\texttt{bool}, \texttt{int}, \texttt{real}, \texttt{string}, \texttt{char}, \texttt{word}, \texttt{list}, \texttt{ref}, \texttt{exn}\}$$

The members of $T_0$ are type names, not type constructors; for convenience we have used type-constructor identifiers to stand also for the type names which are bound to them in the initial static type environment $TE_0$. Of these type names, list and ref have arity 1, the rest have arity 0; all except exn and real admit equality. Finally, $E_0 = (SE_0, TE_0, VE_0)$, where $SE_0 = \{\}$, while $TE_0$ and $VE_0$ are shown in Figures 24 and 25, respectively.

| $tycon$ | $\mapsto$ | ( $\theta$, | $\{vid_1 \mapsto (\sigma_1, is_1), \ldots, vid_n \mapsto (\sigma_n, is_n)\}$ ) | $(n \geq 0)$ |
|---|---|---|---|---|
| unit | $\mapsto$ | ( $\Lambda().\{\}$, | $\{\}$ ) | |
| bool | $\mapsto$ | ( bool, | $\{\texttt{true} \mapsto (\texttt{bool}, c), \texttt{false} \mapsto (\texttt{bool}, c)\}$ ) | |
| int | $\mapsto$ | ( int, | $\{\}$ ) | |
| word | $\mapsto$ | ( word, | $\{\}$ ) | |
| real | $\mapsto$ | ( real, | $\{\}$ ) | |
| string | $\mapsto$ | ( string, | $\{\}$ ) | |
| char | $\mapsto$ | ( char, | $\{\}$ ) | |
| list | $\mapsto$ | ( list, | $\{\texttt{nil} \mapsto (\forall\texttt{'a . 'a list}, c),$ | |
| | | | $\texttt{::} \mapsto (\forall\texttt{'a . 'a} * \texttt{'a list} \to \texttt{'a list}, c)\}$ ) | |
| ref | $\mapsto$ | ( ref, | $\{\texttt{ref} \mapsto (\forall \texttt{'a . 'a} \to \texttt{'a ref}, c)\}$ ) | |
| exn | $\mapsto$ | ( exn, | $\{\}$ ) | |

Figure 24: Static $TE_0$

| NONFIX | | | INFIX | |
|---|---|---|---|---|
| $vid$ | $\mapsto$ | $(\sigma, is)$ | $vid \quad \mapsto \quad (\sigma, is)$ | |
| ref | $\mapsto$ | $(\forall \texttt{'a . 'a} \to \texttt{'a ref}, c)$ | Precedence 5, right associative : | |
| nil | $\mapsto$ | $(\forall\texttt{'a. 'a list}, c)$ | $\texttt{::} \quad \mapsto \quad (\forall\texttt{'a.'a} * \texttt{'a list} \to \texttt{'a list}, c)$ | |
| true | $\mapsto$ | $(\texttt{bool}, c)$ | Precedence 4, left associative : | |
| false | $\mapsto$ | $(\texttt{bool}, c)$ | $\texttt{=} \quad \mapsto \quad (\forall\texttt{''a. ''a} * \texttt{''a} \to \texttt{bool}, v)$ | |
| Match | $\mapsto$ | $(\texttt{exn}, e)$ | Precedence 3, left associative : | |
| Bind | $\mapsto$ | $(\texttt{exn}, e)$ | $\texttt{:=} \quad \mapsto \quad (\forall\texttt{'a. 'a ref} * \texttt{'a} \to \{\}, v)$ | |

Note: In type schemes we have taken the liberty of writing $ty_1 * ty_2$ in place of $\{1 \mapsto ty_1, 2 \mapsto ty_2\}$.

Figure 25: Static $VE_0$

# D    Appendix: The Initial Dynamic Basis

We shall indicate components of the initial basis by the subscript 0. The initial dynamic basis is $B_0 = F_0, G_0, E_0$, where $F_0 = \{\}$, $G_0 = \{\}$ and $E_0 = (SE_0, TE_0, VE_0)$, where $SE_0 = \{\}$, $TE_0$ is shown in Figure 26 and

$$VE_0 = \{ \texttt{=} \mapsto (\texttt{=}, \text{v}), \ \texttt{:=} \mapsto (\texttt{:=}, \text{v}), \texttt{Match} \mapsto (\texttt{Match}, \text{e}), \texttt{Bind} \mapsto (\texttt{Bind}, \text{e}),$$
$$\texttt{true} \mapsto (\texttt{true}, \text{c}), \texttt{false} \mapsto (\texttt{false}, \text{c}),$$
$$\texttt{nil} \mapsto (\texttt{nil}, \text{c}), \texttt{::} \mapsto (\texttt{::}, \text{c}), \texttt{ref} \mapsto (\texttt{ref}, \text{c})\}.$$

| $tycon$ | $\mapsto$ | $\{vid_1 \mapsto (v_1, is_1), \ldots, vid_n \mapsto (v_n, is_n)\} \quad (n \geq 0)$ |
|---:|:---:|:---|
| unit | $\mapsto$ | $\{\}$ |
| bool | $\mapsto$ | $\{\texttt{true} \mapsto (\texttt{true}, \text{c}), \texttt{false} \mapsto (\texttt{false}, \text{c})\}$ |
| int | $\mapsto$ | $\{\}$ |
| word | $\mapsto$ | $\{\}$ |
| real | $\mapsto$ | $\{\}$ |
| string | $\mapsto$ | $\{\}$ |
| char | $\mapsto$ | $\{\}$ |
| list | $\mapsto$ | $\{\texttt{nil} \mapsto (\texttt{nil}, \text{c}), \texttt{::} \mapsto (\texttt{::}, \text{c})\}$ |
| ref | $\mapsto$ | $\{\texttt{ref} \mapsto (\texttt{ref}, \text{c})\}$ |
| exn | $\mapsto$ | $\{\}$ |

Figure 26: Dynamic $TE_0$

# E  Overloading

Two forms of overloading are available:

- Certain special constants are overloaded. For example, 0w5 may have type word or some other type, depending on the surrounding program text;

- Certain operators are overloaded. For example, + may have type int * int → int or real * real → real, depending on the surrounding program text;

Programmers cannot define their own overloaded constants or operators.

Although a formal treatment of overloading is outside the scope of this document, we do give a complete list of the overloaded operators and of types with overloaded special constants. This list is consistent with the Basis Library[18].

Every overloaded constant and value identifier has among its types a *default type*, which is assigned to it, when the surrounding text does not resolve the overloading. For this purpose, the surrounding text is no larger than the smallest enclosing structure-level declaration; an implementation may require that a smaller context determines the type.

## E.1  Overloaded special constants

Libraries may extend the set $T_0$ of Appendix C with additional type names. Thereafter, certain subsets of $T_0$ have a special significance; they are called *overloading classes* and they are:

| | | |
|---|---|---|
| Int | ⊇ | {int} |
| Real | ⊇ | {real} |
| Word | ⊇ | {word} |
| String | ⊇ | {string} |
| Char | ⊇ | {char} |
| WordInt | = | Word ∪ Int |
| RealInt | = | Real ∪ Int |
| Num | = | Word ∪ Real ∪ Int |
| NumTxt | = | Word ∪ Real ∪ Int ∪ String ∪ Char |

Among these, the five first (Int, Real, Word, String and Char) are said to be *basic*; the remaining are said to be *composite*. The reason that the basic classes are specified using ⊇ rather than = is that libraries may extend each of the basic overloading classes with further type names. Special constants are overloaded within each of the basic overloading classes. However, the basic overloading classes must be arranged so that every special constant can be assigned types from at most one of the basic overloading classes. For example, to 0w5 may be assigned type word, or some other member of Word, depending on the surrounding text. If the surrounding text does not determine the type of the constant, a default type is used. The default types for the five sets are int, real, word, string and char respectively.

|              NONFIX              |              INFIX              |
| --- | --- |
| *var* ↦ set of monotypes | *var* ↦ set of monotypes |
| abs ↦ realint → realint | Precedence 7, left associative : |
| ~ ↦ realint → realint | div ↦ wordint * wordint → wordint |
|  | mod ↦ wordint * wordint → wordint |
|  | * ↦ num * num → num |
|  | / ↦ Real * Real → Real |
|  | Precedence 6, left associative : |
|  | + ↦ num * num → num |
|  | - ↦ num * num → num |
|  | Precedence 4, left associative : |
|  | < ↦ numtxt * numtxt → numtxt |
|  | > ↦ numtxt * numtxt → numtxt |
|  | <= ↦ numtxt * numtxt → numtxt |
|  | >= ↦ numtxt * numtxt → numtxt |

Figure 27: Overloaded identifiers

Once overloading resolution has determined the type of a special constant, it is a compile-time error if the constant does not make sense or does not denote a value within the machine representation chosen for the type. For example, an escape sequence of the form \u$xxxx$ in a string constant of 8-bit characters only makes sense if $xxxx$ denotes a number in the range $[0, 255]$.

## E.2   Overloaded value identifiers

Overloaded identifiers all have identifier status v. An overloaded identifier may be re-bound with any status (v, c and e) but then it is not overloaded within the scope of the binding.

The overloaded identifiers are given in Figure 27. For example, the entry

abs ↦ realint → realint

states that abs may assume one of the types $\{t \to t \mid t \in \text{RealInt}\}$. In general, the same type name must be chosen throughout the entire type of the overloaded operator; thus abs does not have type real → int.

The operator / is overloaded on all members of Real, with default type real * real → real. The default type of any other identifier is that one of its types which contains the type name int. For example, the program   fun double(x) = x + x;   declares a function of type int * int → int, while   fun double(x:real) = x + x;   declares a function of type real * real → real.

The dynamic semantics of the overloaded operators is defined in [18].

# F   Appendix: The Development of ML

This Appendix records the main stages in the development of ML, and the people principally involved. The main emphasis is upon the design of the language; there is also a section devoted to implementation. On the other hand, no attempt is made to record work on applications of the language.

## Origins

ML and its semantic description have evolved over a period of about twenty years. It is a fusion of many ideas from many people; in this appendix we try to record and to acknowledge the important precursors of its ideas, the important influences upon it, and the important contributions to its design, implementation and semantic description.

ML, which stands for *meta language*, was conceived as a medium for finding and performing proofs in a formal logical system. This application was the focus of the initial design effort, by Robin Milner in collaboration first with Malcolm Newey and Lockwood Morris, then with Michael Gordon and Christopher Wadsworth [20]. The intended application to proof affected the design considerably. Higher order functions in full generality seemed necessary for programming proof tactics and strategies, and also a robust type system (see below). At the same time, imperative features were important for practical reasons; no-one had experience of large useful programs written in a pure functional style. In particular, an exception-raising mechanism was highly desirable for the natural presentation of tactics.

The full definition of this first version of ML was included in a book [19] which describes LCF, the proof system which ML was designed to support. The details of how the proof application exerted an influence on design is reported by Milner [39]. Other early influences were the applicative languages already in use in Artificial Intelligence, principally LISP [36], ISWIM [28] and POP2 [10].

## Polymorphic types

The polymorphic type discipline and the associated type-assignment algorithm were prompted by the need for security; it is vital to know that when a program produces an object which it claims to be a theorem, then it is indeed a theorem. A type discipline provides the security, but a polymorphic discipline also permits considerable flexibility.

The key ideas of the type discipline were evolved in combinatory logic by Haskell Curry and Roger Hindley, who arrived at different but equivalent algorithms for computing principal type schemes. Curry's [14] algorithm was by equation-solving; Hindley [26] used the unification algorithm of Alan Robinson [48] and also presented the precursor of our type inference system. James Morris [43] independently gave an equation-solving algorithm very similar to Curry's. The idea of an algorithm for finding principal type schemes is very natural and may well have been known earlier. Roger Hindley has pointed out that

Carew Meredith's inference rule for propositional logic called Condensed Detachment, defined in the early 1950s, clearly suggests that he knew such an algorithm [37].

Milner [38], during the design of ML, rediscovered principal types and their calculation by unification, for a language (slightly richer than combinatory logic) containing local declarations. He and Damas [15] presented the ML type inference systems following Hindley's style. Damas [16], using ideas from Michael Gordon, also devised the first mathematical treatment of polymorphism in the presence of references and assignment. Tofte [54] produced a different scheme employing so-called *imperative types*, which was adopted in the original version of the language. This approach has been superseded in the present language by a simpler scheme, suggested by Tofte [54], Andrew Wright [57], and Xavier Leroy [29], according to which polymorphic bindings are restricted to non-expansive expressions.

## Refinement of the Core Language

Two movements led to the re-design of ML. One was the work of Rod Burstall and his group on specifications, crystallised in the specification language CLEAR [11] and in the functional programming language HOPE [12]; the latter was for expressing executable specifications. The outcome of this work which is relevant here was twofold. First, there were elegant programming features in HOPE, particularly pattern matching and clausal function definitions; second, there were ideas on modular construction of specifications, using signatures in the interfaces. A smaller but significant movement was by Luca Cardelli, who extended the data-type repertoire in ML by adding named records and variant types.

In 1983, Milner (prompted by Bernard Sufrin) wrote the first draft of a standard form of ML attempting to unite these ideas; over the next three years it evolved into the Standard ML core language. Notable here was the harmony found among polymorphism, HOPE patterns and Cardelli records, and the nice generalisations of ML exceptions due to ideas from Alan Mycroft, Brian Monahan and Don Sannella. A simple stream-based I/O mechanism was developed from ideas of Cardelli by Milner and Harper. The Standard ML core language is described in detail in a composite report [23] which also contains a description of the I/O mechanism and MacQueen's proposal for program modules (see later for discussion of this). Since then only few changes to the core language have occurred. Milner proposed equality types, and these were added, together with a few minor adjustments [40]. The last development before the 1990 Definition was in the exception mechanism, by MacQueen using an idea from Burstall [3]; it harmonized the ideas of exception and data type construction.

## Modules

Besides contributory ideas to the core language, HOPE [12] contained a simple notion of program module. The most important and original feature of ML modules, however, stems from the work on parameterised specifications in CLEAR [11]. MacQueen, who was a member of Burstall's group at the time, designed [34] a new parametric module feature for HOPE inspired by the CLEAR work. He later extended the parameterisation ideas by a novel method of specifying sharing of components among the structure parameters of a functor, and produced a draft design which accommodated features already present in ML – in particular the polymorphic type system. This design was discussed in detail at Edinburgh, leading to MacQueen's first report on modules [23].

Thereafter, the design came under close scrutiny through a draft operational static semantics and prototype implementation of it by Harper, through Kevin Mitchell's implementation of the evaluation, through a denotational semantics written by Don Sannella, and then through further work on operational semantics by Harper, Milner, and Tofte. (More is said about this in the later section on Semantics.) In all of this work the central ideas withstood scrutiny, while it also became clear that there were gaps in the design and ambiguities in interpretation. (An example of a gap was the inability to specify sharing between a functor argument structure and its result structure; an example of an ambiguity was the question of whether sharing exists in a structure over and above what is specified in the signature expression which accompanies its declaration.)

Much discussion ensued; it was possible for a wider group to comment on modules through using Harper's prototype implementation, while Harper, Milner and Tofte gained understanding during development of this semantics. In parallel, Sannella and Tarlecki explored the implications of modules for the methodology of program development [49]. Tofte, in his thesis [53], proved several technical properties of modules in a skeletal language, which generated considerable confidence in this design. A key point in this development was the proof of the existence of principal signatures, and, in the careful distinction between the notion of *enrichment* of structures, which allows more polymorphism and more components, and *realisation* which allows more sharing.

At a meeting in Edinburgh in 1987 a choice of two designs was presented, hinging upon whether or not a functor application should coerce its actual argument to its argument signature. The meeting chose coercion, and thereafter the production of Section 5 of this report – the static semantics of modules – was a matter of detailed care. That section is undoubtedly the most original and demanding part of this semantics, just as the ideas of MacQueen upon which it is based are the most far-reaching extension to the original design of ML.

Considerable experience was gained in implementing, programming with, and teaching the language during the nearly ten years since the definition was first published. Based on this experience a number of design decisions were revisited at a meeting of the authors in Cambridge at the end of 1995. At this meeting it was decided to make several modest, but significant, changes to the language in order to simplify the semantics and to correct some shortcomings that had come to light. The most important of these changes was the replacement of the imperative type discipline by the so-called value restriction (discussed above), the elimination of structure sharing as a separate concept from type sharing, and the introduction of the closely connected mechanisms of opaque signature matching and type abbreviations in signatures. An important impetus for these changes to the modules language was the work of Leroy [30], and Harper and Lillibridge [21] on the type-theoretic interpretation of modules (described below).

## Implementation

The first implementation of ML was by Malcolm Newey, Lockwood Morris and Robin Milner in 1974, for the DEC10. Later Mike Gordon and Chris Wadsworth joined; their work was mainly in specialising ML towards machine-assisted reasoning. Around 1980 Luca Cardelli implemented a version on VAX; his work was later extended by Alan Mycroft, Kevin Mitchell and John Scott. This version contained one or two new data-type features, and was based upon the *Functional Abstract Machine (FAM)*, a virtual machine which has been a considerable stimulus to later implementation. By providing a reasonably efficient implementation, this work enabled the language to be taught to students; this, in turn, prompted the idea that it could become a useful general purpose language.

In Gothenburg, an implementation was developed by Lennart Augustsson and Thomas Johnsson in 1982, using lazy evaluation rather than call-by-value; the result was called *Lazy ML* and is described in [6]. This work is part of continuing research in many places on implementation of lazy evaluation in pure functional languages. But for ML, which includes exceptions and assignment, the emphasis has been mainly upon strict evaluation (call-by-value).

In Cambridge, in the early 1980s, Larry Paulson made considerable improvements to the Edinburgh ML compiler, as part of his wider programme of improving *Edinburgh LCF* to become *Cambridge LCF* [46]. This system has supported larger proofs than the Edinburgh system, and with greater convenience; in particular, the compiled ML code ran four to five times faster.

Around the same time Gérard Huet at INRIA (Versailles) adapted ML to Maclisp on Multics, again for use in machine-assisted proof. There was close collaboration between INRIA and Cambridge in this period. ML has undergone a separate development in the group at INRIA on the *CAML* language [13]. Work on *CAML* included the development of several extensions to the core language, notably updatable fields in record types, values with dynamic types, support for lazy evaluation, and handling of embedded languages with user-defined syntax. It did not, however, include modules.

The first implementation of the Standard ML core language was by Mitchell, Mycroft and Scott at Edinburgh, around 1984. The prototype implementation of modules, before that part of the language settled down, was done in 1985-6; Mitchell dealt with evaluation, while Harper tackled the elaboration (or 'signature checking') which raised problems of a kind not previously encountered. Harper's implementation employed a form of unification that was later adopted in the static semantics of modules.

At around the same time the *Poly/ML* implementation began with a suggestion from Mike Gordon that an interesting application of Matthews' Poly language would be to implement Standard ML. Important experience was gained through Matthews' early implementation of the core language, followed by several versions of the modules language as they were devised. *Poly/ML* features arbitrary precision arithmetic, a process package, and a windowing system. Considerable experience has been gained with the compiler, notably by Larry Paulson at Cambridge and by Abstract Hardware Limited (AHL).

The *Standard ML of New Jersey (SML/NJ)* system has been in active development since 1986 [5,2]. Initially started by David MacQueen at Bell Laboratories and Andrew Appel at Princeton University, the project has also benefited from significant contributions by Matthias Blume, Emden Gansner, Lal George, John Reppy and Zhong Shao. *SML/NJ* is a robust and complete environment for Standard ML that supports the implementation of large software systems and generates efficient code for a number of different hardware and software platforms. *SML/NJ* also serves as a laboratory for compiler research: in implementations of module systems for ML; code optimization based on continuation-passing style; efficient pattern matching; and very fast heap allocation and garbage collection. Dozens of researchers have contributed to the development of the compiler, in such areas as efficient closure representations, first-class continuations, type-directed compilation, concurrent programming, portable code generators, separate compilation, and register allocation. *SML/NJ* has also been widely used to explore extending SML with concurrency features.

In 1989, Mads Tofte, Nick Rothwell and David N. Turner started work on the *ML Kit Compiler* in Edinburgh. The *ML Kit* is a direct translation of the 1990 Definition into a collection of Standard ML modules, emphasis being on clarity rather than efficiency. During 1992 and 1993, Version 1 of the *ML Kit* was completed, mostly through the work of Nick Rothwell at Edinburgh and Lars Birkedal at DIKU[9]. In 1994, region inference was added to the *ML Kit*, by Mads Tofte. Lars Birkedal wrote a region-based C-code generator and a runtime system in C. In 1995, Martin Elsman and Niels Hallenberg extended this work to generate native code for the HP PA-RISC architecture.

Harlequin Ltd. began the implementation of a commercial compiler in 1990. The *MLWorks* system is a fully-featured graphical programming environment, including an interactive debugger, inspector, browser, extensive profiling facilities, separate compilation and delivery, a foreign-language interface, and libraries for threads and windowing systems.

*Caml Light*, a lightweight reimplementation of *CAML* released in 1991, added a simple module system in the style of Modula-2, targeted towards separate compilation of modules: structures and signatures are identified with files, functors and multiple views of a structure are not supported. These were added in the *Caml Special Light* implementation in 1995, while preserving the support for separate compilation. *Caml Special Light* and the present version of Standard ML share several important simplifications, such as the value restriction on polymorphism, type definitions in signatures, and the lack of support for structure sharing. The static semantics for *Caml Special Light* is based on the type-theoretic properties of dependent function types (functor signatures) and manifest types (type definitions in signatures) [30].

*Moscow ML* is an implementation of core Standard ML, created in 1994 by Sergei Romanenko in Moscow and Peter Sestoft in Copenhagen. The *Caml Light* system was used to implement the dynamic semantics, and the ML Kit guided the implementation of the static semantics. The result is a compact and robust implementation, suitable for teaching.

The *TIL (Typed Intermediate Languages)* compiler developed at Carnegie Mellon University by Greg Morrisett, David Tarditi, Perry Cheng, Chris Stone, Robert Harper, and Peter Lee demonstrates the use of types in compilation. All but the last few stages of *TIL* are expressed as type-directed and type-preserving transforms. Types are used at run time to support unboxed, untagged data representations and natural calling conventions in the presence of variable types and garbage collection. *TIL* employs a wide variety of conventional functional language optimizations found in other SML compilers, as well as a set of loop-oriented optimizations. A description of the compiler and an analysis of its performance appears in [52].

Other currently active implementations are by Michael Hedlund at the Rutherford-Appleton Laboratory, by Robert Duncan, Simon Nichols and Aaron Sloman at the University of Sussex (*POPLOG*) and by Malcolm Newey and his group at the Australian National University.

## Semantics

The description of the first version of ML [19] was informal, and in an operational style; around the same time a denotational semantics was written, but never published, by Mike Gordon and Robin Milner. Meanwhile structured operational semantics, presented as an inference system, was gaining credence as a tractable medium. This originates with the reduction rules of λ-calculus, but was developed more widely through the work of Plotkin [47], and also by Milner. This was at first only used for dynamic semantics, but later the benefit of using inference systems for both static and dynamic semantics became apparent. This advantage was realised when Gilles Kahn and his group at INRIA were able to execute early versions of both forms of semantics for the ML core language using their Typol system [17]. The static and dynamic semantics of the core language reached a final form mostly through work by Tofte and Milner.

The modules of ML presented little difficulty as far as dynamic semantics is concerned, but the static semantics of modules was a concerted effort by several people. MacQueen's original informal description [23] was the starting point; Sannella wrote a denotational semantics for several versions, which showed that several issues had not been settled by the informal description. Robert Harper, while writing the first implementation of modules, made the first draft of the static semantics. Harper's version made clear the importance of structure names; work by Milner and Tofte introduced further ideas including realisation; thereafter a concerted effort by all three led to several suggestions for modification of the language, and a small range of alternative interpretations; these were assessed in discussion with MacQueen, and more widely with the principal users of the language, and an agreed form was reached.

Concurrently with the formulation of the Definition of Standard ML, Harper and Mitchell took up the challenge adumbrated by MacQueen [33] to find a type-theoretic interpretation of Standard ML [25]. This work led to the formulation of the XML language, an explicitly-typed λ-calculus that captured many aspects of Standard ML. Although incomplete, their approach formed the basis for a number of subsequent studies, including the work of Harper and Lillibridge [21] and Leroy [30] on the type-theoretic interpretation of modules. This work influenced the decision to revise the language, and culminated in a type-theoretic interpretation of the present language by Harper and Stone [51]. The TIL/ML compiler (described above) is based directly on this interpretation.

There is no doubt that the interaction between design and semantic description of modules has been one of the most striking phases in the entire language development, leading (in the opinion of those involved) to a high degree of confidence both in the language and in the semantics.

## Program Libraries

During 1989-1991, Dave Berry produced the first program library for Standard ML[7,8]. The *SML/NJ* system is distributed with a rich library organised by Emden Gansner and John Reppy; this library was the starting point for the SML Basis Library . The *SML Basis Library*[18] has been developed over the past three years in a partnership between the SML/NJ effort, *MLWorks*, and *Moscow ML*. The resulting library is a much improved and extended replacement of the initial basis defined in the 1990 Definition of Standard ML.

# G   Appendix: What is New?

This appendix gives an overview of how the present Definition differs from the 1990 Definition of Standard ML[42]. For the purpose of this appendix, we write SML '90 for the language defined by the 1990 Definition and SML '97 for the present language. For each major change, we give its rationale and an overview of its practical implications. Also, the index (page 101 ff.) may be used for locating changes.

## G.1   Type Abbreviations in Signatures

There are cases of type sharing which cannot be expressed in SML '90 signatures although they arise in structures. For example, there is no SML '90 signature which precisely describes the relationship between s and t in

```
structure a =
struct
  datatype s = C
  type t = s * s
end
```

In SML '97, one can write *type abbreviations* in signatures, e.g.,

```
signature A =
sig
  type s
  type t = s * s
end
```

The need for type abbreviations in signatures was clear when SML '90 was defined. However, type abbreviations were not included since, in the presence of both structure sharing and type abbreviations, principal signatures do not exist[41] – and the SML '90 Definition depended strongly upon the notion of principal signature. Subsequently, Harper's and Lillibridge's work on translucent sums[22] and Leroy's work on modules[30] showed that, in the absence of structure sharing and certain other features of the SML '90 signatures, type abbreviations in signatures are possible. Type abbreviations in signatures were implemented by David MacQueen in *SML/NJ* 0.93 and by Xavier Leroy in *Caml Special Light*[31].

In SML '97, structure sharing has been removed (see Section G.3 below). Type abbreviations are not included directly, but they arise as a derived form, as follows. First, a new form of signature expression is allowed:

$$sigexp \text{ \textbf{where type} } tyvarseq \ longtycon = ty$$

Here *longtycon* has to be specified by *sigexp*. The type expression *ty* may refer to type constructors which are present in the basis in which the whole signature expression is elaborated, but not to type constructors specified in *sigexp*.

The effect of the `where type` is, roughly speaking, to instantiate *longtycon* to *ty*. For example, the following sequence of declarations is legal:

```
signature SIG1 = sig type t; val x: t end;
signature SIG2 = SIG1 where type t = int*int;
structure S1: SIG1 = struct type t = real; val x = 1.0 end;
structure S2: SIG2 = struct type t = int*int; val x = (5, 7) end;
```

Next, a type abbreviation is a derived form. For example, `type u = t*t` is equivalent to `include sig type u end where type u = t*t` . In SML '97 it is allowed to include an arbitrary signature expression, not just a signature identifier.

## G.2   Opaque Signature Matching

In imposing a signature on a structure, one often wants the types of the resulting structure to be "abstract" in order to hide their implementation. (Signature matching in SML '90 hides components, but does not hide type sharing.) MacQueen originally suggested and implemented an `abstraction` declaration for this purpose[32]. In the Commentary[41] it was pointed out that the issue is the semantics of matching. SML '97 provides two kinds of matching, as new forms of structure expression:

$$strexp \quad : \quad sigexp$$

$$strexp \quad :> \quad sigexp$$

The first (`:`) is the SML '90 signature matching; the second (`:>`) is *opaque matching*. Opaque matching can be applied to the result structure of a functor; thus it is more general than MacQueen's `abstraction` declaration. In CAML Special Light, all signature matching is opaque.

With opaque matching, types in the resulting structure will be abstract, to precisely the degree expressed in *sigexp*. Thus

```
signature Sig =
  sig
    type t = int
    val x: t
    type u
    val y: u
  end;
structure S1:> Sig =
  struct type t = int
         val x = 3
         type u = real
         val y = 3.0
  end
val r = S1.x + 1
```

is legal, but a subsequent declaration `val s = S1.y + 1.5` will fail to elaborate. Similarly, consider the functor declaration:

```
functor Dict(type t; val leq: t*t->int):>
            sig type u = t*t
                type 'a dict
            end =
   struct
     type u = t*t
     type 'a dict = (t * 'a) list
   end
```

When applied, `Dict` will propagate the identity of the type `t` from argument to result, but it will produce a fresh `dict` type upon each application.

Types which are specified as "abstract" in a opaque functor result signature give rise to generation of fresh type names upon each application of the functor, even if the functor body is a constant structure. For example, after the elaboration of

```
structure A = struct type t = int end
functor f():> sig type t end = A
structure B = f()
        and C = f();
```

the two types `B.t` and `C.t` are different.

## G.3   Sharing

Structure sharing is a key idea in MacQueen's original Modules design[32]. The theoretical aspects of structure sharing have been the subject of considerable research attention[24,53, 1,55,35]. However, judging from experience, structure sharing is not often used in its full generality, namely to ensure identity of values. Furthermore, experience from teaching suggests that the structure sharing concept is somewhat hard to grasp. Finally, the semantic accounts of structure sharing that have been proposed are rather complicated.

The static semantics of SML '97 has no notion of structure sharing. However, SML '97 does provide a weaker form of structure sharing constraints, in which structure sharing is regarded as a derived form, equivalent to a collection of type sharing constraints.

### G.3.1   Type Sharing

In SML '90, a type sharing constraint `sharing type` $longtycon_1 = \cdots = longtycon_n$ was an admissible form of specification. In SML '97 such a constraint does not stand by itself as a specification, but may be used to qualify a specification. Thus there is a new form of specification, which we shall call a *qualified* specification:

$$spec\ \texttt{sharing type}\ longtycon_1 = \cdots = longtycon_n$$

Here the long type constructors have to be specified by *spec*. The type constructors may have been specified by `type`, `eqtype` or `datatype` specifications, or indirectly through signature identifiers and `include`. In order for the specification to be legal, all the type constructors must denote flexible type names. More precisely, let $B$ be the basis in which the qualified specification is elaborated. Let us say that a type name $t$ is *rigid (in B)* if $t \in T$ of $B$ and that $t$ is *flexible (in B)* otherwise. For example `int` is rigid in the initial basis and every datatype declaration introduces additional rigid type names into the basis. For the qualified specification to elaborate in basis $B$, it is required that each *longtycon$_i$* denotes a type name which is flexible in $B$. In particular, no *longtycon$_i$* may denote a type function which is not also a type name (e.g., a *longtycon* must not denote $\Lambda().s * s$).

For example, the two signature expressions

```
sig                          sig
  type s                       type s
  type t                       datatype t = C
  sharing type s = t           sharing type s = t
end                          end
```

are both legal. By contrast, the signature expressions

```
sig                          sig
  type s                       type s = int
  type t = s*s                 datatype t = C
  sharing type s = t           sharing type s = t
end                          end
```

are both illegal.

## G.3.2   The equality attribute of specified types

If *spec* `sharing type` *longtycon*$_1$ $= \cdots =$ *longtycon*$_n$ elaborates successfully, then all $n$ type constructors will thereafter denote the same type name. This type name will admit equality, if *spec* associates an equality type name with one of the type constructors. Thus

```
eqtype t
type u
sharing type t = u
```

is legal and both t and u are equality types after the sharing qualification. The mechanism for inferring equality attributes for datatype specifications is the same as for inferring equality attributes for datatype declarations. Thus the specification

```
datatype answer = YES | NO
datatype 'a option = Some of 'a | None
```

specifies two equality types. Every specification of the form `datatype` *datdesc* introduces one type name for each type constructor described by *datdesc*. The equality attribute of such a type name is determined at the point where the specification occurs. Thus, in

```
type s
datatype t  = C of s
```

the type name associated with `t` will not admit equality, even if `s` later is instantiated to an equality type. Type names associated with datatype specifications can be instantiated to other type names by subsequent `type sharing` or `where type` qualifications. In this case, no effort is made to ban type environments that do not respect equality. For example,

```
sig
   eqtype s
   datatype t = C of int -> int
   sharing type s = t
end
```

is legal in SML '97, even though it cannot be matched by any real structure.

### G.3.3   Structure Sharing

For convenience, structure sharing constraints are provided, but only as a shorthand for type sharing constraints. There is a derived form of specification

$$spec \; \texttt{sharing} \; longstrid_1 = \cdots = longstrid_k \qquad (k \geq 2)$$

Here *spec* must specify $longstrid_1, \ldots, longstrid_k$. The equivalent form consists of *spec* qualified by all the type sharing constraints

$$\texttt{sharing type} \; longstrid_i.longtycon = longstrid_j.longtycon$$

$(1 \leq i < j \leq k)$ such that both $longstrid_i.longtycon$ and $longstrid_j.longtycon$ are specified by *spec*.

In SML '90, structure sharing constraints are transitive, but in SML '97 they are not. For example,

```
structure A: sig type t end
structure B: sig end
structure C: sig type t end
sharing A=B=C
```

induces type sharing on `t`, whereas

```
structure A: sig type t end
structure B: sig end
structure C: sig type t end
sharing A=B sharing B=C
```

induces no type sharing. Thus a structure sharing constraint in some cases induces less sharing in SML '97 than in SML '90.

Next, SML '97 does not allow structure sharing equations which refer to "external" structures. For example, the program

```
structure A= struct end;
signature SIG = sig structure B : sig end
                    sharing A = B
              end;
```

is not legal in SML '97, because the sharing constraint now only qualifies the specification `structure B: sig end`, which does not specify `A`. Thus not all legal SML '90 signatures are legal in SML '97.

The removal of structure sharing has a dramatic simplifying effect on the semantics. Most importantly, the elaboration rules can be made monogenic (i.e., "deterministic"), up to renaming of new type names. The need for the notion of principal signature (and even equality-principal signature) disappears. The notions of structure name, structure consistency and well-formed signature are no longer required. The notion of cover can be deleted. Only one kind of realisation, namely type realisation, remains. The notion of type-explication has been removed, since it can be proved that signatures automatically are type-explicit in the revised language.

## G.4   Value Polymorphism

The imperative types of SML '90 were somewhat subtle, and they propagated into signatures in an unpleasant way. Experiments on existing code suggest that the power of imperative types is rarely used fully and that *value polymorphism*, which can in fact be seen as a restriction of the imperative type discipline, usually suffices[57]. With value polymorphism, there is only one kind of type variable. The definition of non-expansive expressions (see G.13 below) is relaxed to admit more expressions. In a declaration

$$\text{val } x \text{ = } exp$$

the variable $x$ will only be given a non-trivial polymorphic type scheme (i.e., a type scheme which is not also a type) if $exp$ is non-expansive. This applies even if there is no application of `ref` in the entire program.

Example: in the declaration `val x = []  @ []`, x can be assigned type `'a list`, but not the type scheme $\forall$`'a.'a list` (since `[]  @ []` is an expansive expression). Consequently, `(1::x, true::x)` will not elaborate in the scope of the declaration. Also, if the declaration appears at top level, the compiler may refuse elaboration due to a top-level free type variable (see G.8). Thus the top-level phrase `[]  @ []` may fail, since it abbreviates `val it = []  @ []`. But of course it will not fail if a monotype is explicitly ascribed, e.g. `[]  @ []:int list`.

On the other hand, in `fun f() = []  @ []` (or `val f = fn () => []  @ []`), f can be assigned type scheme $\forall$`'a.unit` $\to$ `'a list` so that, for example, `(1::f(),true::f())`

elaborates. This transformation ($\eta$-conversion) often gives the desired polymorphism. But beware that $\eta$-conversion can change the meaning of the program, if *exp* does not terminate or has side-effects.

## G.5 Identifier Status

The 1990 Definition treated identifier status informally (in Section 2.4); a fuller definition was given in the Commentary[41, Appendix B]. However, some problems with the handling of exception constructors remained[27, Sect. 10.3].

In the present document, we have collapsed the three identifier classes Var, ExCon and Con into a single class, VId, of *value identifiers*. The semantic objects *VE* previously called variable environments are replaced by *value environments*. A value environment maps value identifiers to pairs of the form $(o, \textit{is})$, where $o$ is some semantic object and *is* is an *identifier status* ($\textit{is} \in \{\mathtt{v}, \mathtt{c}, \mathtt{e}\}$) indicating whether the identifier should be regarded as a value variable ($\mathtt{v}$), a value constructor ($\mathtt{c}$) or an exception constructor ($\mathtt{e}$). These changes have been carried out both in the static and in the dynamic semantics, for both Core and Modules. Thus the assignment of identifier status is incorporated formally in the present Definition.

The definition of enrichment has been modified to allow an identifier that has been specified as a value to be matched by a value constructor or an exception constructor. However, a specification of a value or exception constructor must be matched by a value or exception constructor, respectively.

Thus, the status descriptor says more than just what the lexical status of the identifier is — it is a statement about the value in the corresponding dynamic environment: if the status of *id* in the static environment is $\mathtt{c}$, then the value in a matching dynamic environment must be a value constructor. Similarly, if the status of *id* in the static environment is $\mathtt{e}$, then the value in a matching dynamic environment must be an exception name. If the status of *id* is just $\mathtt{v}$, however, the corresponding value in the dynamic environment can be any kind of value (of the appropriate type), including a value constructor and an exception name.

The exception environment (*EE*) has been deleted from the semantics, since it is no longer required for the definition of enrichment. Also, the constructor environment *CE* in the static semantics has been replaced by a value environment in which every identifier has status $\mathtt{c}$.

The new handling of identifier status admits some `val rec` declarations that were illegal in SML '90 (see the comment to Rule 26).

## G.6 Replication of Datatypes

SML '97 allows *datatype replication*, i.e. declarations and specifications of the form

$$\mathtt{datatype}\ \textit{tycon} = \mathtt{datatype}\ \textit{longtycon}$$

When elaborated, this binds type constructor *tycon* to the entire type structure (value constructors included) to which *longtycon* is bound in the context. Datatype replication does not generate a new datatype: the original and the replicated datatype share.

Here is an example of a use of the new construct:

```
signature MYBOOL =
sig
  type bool
  val xor: bool * bool -> bool
end;
structure MyBool: MYBOOL =
struct
  datatype bool = datatype bool (* from the initial basis *)
  fun xor(true, false) = true
    | xor(false, true) = true
    | xor _ = false
end;
val x = MyBool.xor(true, false);
```

Here MyBool.xor(true, false) evaluates to true. Note the use of transparent signature matching; had opaque matching been used instead, the declaration of x would not have elaborated.

A datatype replication implicitly introduces the value constructors of *longtycon* into the current scope. This is significant for signature matching. For example, the following program is legal:

```
datatype t0 = C;
structure A : sig type t val C: t end =
  struct
    datatype t = datatype t0
  end;
```

Note that C is specified as a value in the signature; the datatype replication copies the value environment of t0 into the structure and that is why the structure contains the required C value.

To make it possible for datatype replication to copy value environments associated with type constructors, the dynamic semantics has been modified so that environments now contain a *TE* component (see Figure 13, page 38). Further, in the dynamic semantics of modules, the ↓ operation, which is used for cutting down structures when they are matched against signatures, has been extended to cover the *TE* component (see page 48). In the above example, the value environment assigned to A.t will be empty, signifying that the type has no value constructors. Had the signature instead been

```
sig datatype t val C: t end
```

then the signature matching would have assigned `A.t` a value environment with domain {C}, indicating that `A.t` has value constructor `C`.

When the datatype replication is used as a specification, *longtycon* can refer to a datatype which has been introduced either by declaration or by specification. Here is an example of the former:

```
datatype t = C | D;
signature SIG =
sig
  datatype t = datatype t (* replication is not recursive! *)
  val f: t -> t
end
```

## G.7   Local Datatypes

This change is concerned with expressions of the form `let` *dec* `in` *exp* `end` in which *dec* contains a `datatype` declaration. Let us refer to such a datatype declaration as a *local* datatype declaration. There are two reasons why changes to the handling of local datatype declarations are necessary.

The first is that the rule given for elaboration of `let`-expressions in the 1990 Definition is unsound[27]; the problem has to do with the ability to export type names of locally declared datatypes out of scope.

The second is that the static semantics relies on the following invariant about all contexts, $C$, which arise in elaboration from the initial basis:

$$\text{tynames}\, C \subseteq T \text{ of } C$$

This invariant is used, for example, in the rule for elaborating datatype declarations, where type names are picked "fresh" with respect to $T$ of $C$. As pointed out by Kahrs, the second premise of rule 16 in the 1990 Definition violates the above invariant.

To solve the first problem, the rule for elaborating `let`-expressions (rule 4 in the present document) has been provided with a side-condition which prevents the type of *exp* from containing type names generated by *dec*. For example,

```
let datatype t = C in C end
```

was legal SML '90 but is not legal SML '97.

To solve the second problem, a side-condition has been added in the rule for matches and the rule for `val rec` (rules 14 and 26 of the present document). As a consequence, again fewer programs elaborate. For example, the expression

```
fn x => let datatype t = C
            val _ = if true then x else C
        in 5
        end
```

is not legal SML '97, although it was legal SML '90.

## G.8   Principal Environments

In SML '90, the elaboration rule which allows any *dec* to appear as a *strdec* is

$$\frac{C \text{ of } B \vdash dec \Rightarrow E \quad E \text{ principal for } dec \text{ in } (C \text{ of } B)}{B \vdash dec \Rightarrow E}$$

The side-condition forces the type scheme in $E$ to be as general as possible. However, this side-condition would be undesirably restrictive in SML '97, since the new definition of the Clos operation admits less polymorphism than the one used in SML '90. For example, neither

```
val f = (fn x => x)(fn x => x)
structure A  = struct end
val y = f 7
```

(where the presence of the `structure` declaration forces each `val` declaration to be parsed as a *strdec*), nor

```
structure A: sig val f: int -> int end =
   struct
       val f = (fn x => x)(fn x => x)
   end
```

would be legal in SML '97, if the side-condition were enforced. (A type-checker may at first infer the type $'a \to 'a$ from the declaration of `f`, but since `(fn x => x)(fn x => x)` is expansive, the generalisation to $\forall 'a.'a \to 'a$ is not allowed.) By dropping the side-condition, it becomes possible to have the textual context of a structure-level declaration constrain free type variables to monotypes. Thus both the above examples can be elaborated.

Rather than lifting the notion of principal environments to the modules level, we have chosen to drop the requirement of principality. Since the notion of principal environments is no longer used in the rules, even the definition of principal environments has been removed. In practice, however, type checkers still have to infer types that are as general as possible, since implementations should not reject programs for which successful elaboration is possible.

In order to avoid reporting free type variables to users, rules 87 and 89 require that the environment to which a *topdec* elaborates must not contain free type variables. It is possible to satisfy this side-condition by replacing such type variables by arbitrary monotypes; however, implementers may instead choose to refuse elaboration in such situations.

## G.9   Consistency and Admissibility

The primary purpose of consistency in SML '90 was to allow a very simple elaboration rule for structure sharing. A secondary purpose was to ban any signature which, because it specifies a datatype in inconsistent ways (e.g. with different constructors), can never be matched. With the removal of structure sharing, the primary purpose of consistency has gone away. In our experience, the secondary purpose has turned out not to be very significant in practice. Textual copying of datatype specifications in different signatures is best avoided, since changes in the datatype will have to be done several places. In practice, it is better to specify a datatype in one signature and then access it elsewhere using structure specifications or include. In SML '90 one could specify sharing between a datatype specification and an external (i.e., declared) datatype, and a consistency check was useful in this case. But in SML '97 this form of sharing is not allowed, so there remains no strong reason for preserving consistency; therefore it has been dropped.

In SML '90, admissibility was imposed partly to ensure the existence of principal signatures (which are no longer needed) and partly to ban certain unmatchable signatures. In SML '90, admissibility was the conjunction of well-formedness, cycle-freedom and consistency. Cycle-freedom is no longer relevant, since there is no structure sharing. We have already discussed consistency. Well-formedness of signatures is no longer relevant, but the notion of well-formed type structures is still relevant. It turns out that well-formedness only needs to be checked in one place (in rule 64). Otherwise, well-formedness is preserved by the rules (in a sense which can be made precise). Thus one can avoid a global well-formedness requirement and dispense with admissibility. This we have done.

## G.10 Special Constants

The class of special constants has been extended with word and char constants and with hexadecimal notation. Also, there are additional escape sequences in strings and support for UNICODE characters. See Section 2.2.

## G.11 Comments

A clarification concerning unmatched comment brackets was presented in the Commentary; subsequently, Stefan Kahrs discovered a problem with demanding that an unmatched *) be reported by the compiler. In SML '97, we therefore simply demand that an unmatched (* must be reported by the compiler.

## G.12 Infixed Operators

The rules for associativity of infix operators at the same level of precedence have been modified, to avoid confusion between right- and left-associative operators with the same binding precedence (see Section 2.6).

## G.13 Non-expansive Expressions

The class of non-expansive expressions (Section 4.7) has been extended, to compensate for the loss of polymorphism which value polymorphism entails.

## G.14   Rebinding of built-in identifiers

In SML '97, no *datbind*, *valbind* or *exbind* may bind `true`, `false`, `nil`, `::` or `ref` and
no *datbind* or *exbind* may bind `it` (Section 2.9). Similarly, no *datdesc*, *valdesc* or *exdesc*
may describe `true`, `false`, `nil`, `::` or `ref` and no *datdesc* or *exdesc* may describe `it`
(Section 3.5). These changes are made in order to fix the meaning of derived forms and
to avoid ambiguity in the handling of `ref` in the dynamic semantics of the Core.

## G.15   Grammar for Modules

There are several new derived forms for modules, see Appendix A (Figures 18 and 19).
The grammar for *topdec* has been modified, so that there is no longer any need to put
semicolons at the end of signature and functor declarations. Empty and sequential signature and functor declarations have been removed, as they no longer serve any purpose.
SML '97 has neither functor signature expressions nor functor specifications, since they
could not occur in programs and did not gain wide acceptance

## G.16   Closure Restrictions

Section 3.6 of the 1990 Definition has been deleted.

## G.17   Specifications

`open` and `local` specifications have been criticised on the grounds of programming methodology[4]. Also, they are no longer needed for defining the derived forms for functors and
they conflict with a desire to have all signatures be type-explicit.

   SML '97 therefore admits neither `open` nor `local` in specifications. Moreover, sequential specifications must not specify the same identifier twice. As a consequence, the
definition of type-explication has been removed: type-explication is automatically preserved by elaboration (if one starts in the initial basis) so there is no need to impose
type-explicitness explicitly.

## G.18   Scope of Explicit Type Variables

A binding construct for explicit type variables has been introduced at `val` and `fun` (see
Figure 21). For example, one can declare the polymorphic identity function by

$$\text{fun 'a id(x:'a) = x}$$

   There is no requirement that all explicit type variables be bound by this binding
construct. For those that are not, the scope rules of the 1990 Definition apply. The
explicit binding construct has no impact on the dynamic semantics. In particular, there
are no explicit type abstractions or applications in the dynamic semantics.

## G.19   The Initial Basis

To achieve a clean interface to the new Standard ML Basis Library[18], the initial basis (Appendices C and D) has been cut down to a bare minimum. The present Definition only provides what is necessary in order to define the derived forms and special constants of type `int`, `real`, `word`, `char` and `string`. The following identifiers are no longer defined in the initial basis: `<>`, `^`, `!`, `@`, `Abs`, `arctan`, `chr`, `Chr`, `close_in`, `close_out`, `cos`, `Diff`, `Div`, `end_of_stream`, `exp`, `Exp`, `explode`, `floor`, `Floor`, `implode`, `input`, `instream`, `Interrupt`, `Io`, `ln`, `Ln`, `lookahead`, `map`, `Mod`, `Neg`, `not`, `real` (the coercion function), `rev`, `sin`, `size`, `sqrt`, `Sqrt`, `std_in`, `std_out`, `Sum`, `output`, `outstream`, `Prod`, `Quot`. The corresponding basic values have also been deleted.

## G.20   Overloading

The Standard ML Basis Library[18] rests on an overloading scheme for special constants and pre-defined identifiers. We have adopted this scheme (see Appendix E).

## G.21   Reals

`real` is no longer an equality type and real constants are no longer allowed in patterns. The Basis Library provides IEEE equality operations on reals.

# References

[1] Maria Virginia Aponte. Extending record typing to type parametric modules with sharing. In *Proc. of the Twentieth Annual ACM SIGPLAN-SIGACT Symposium on Principles of Programming Languages (POPL)*, pages 465–478. ACM Press, January 1993.

[2] A. W. Appel and D. B. MacQueen. Standard ML of New Jersey. In *Programming Language Implementation and Logic Programming*, volume 528 of *Lecture Notes in Computer Science*, pages 1–26, New York, N.Y., August 1991. Springer-Verlag.

[3] Andrew Appel, David MacQueen, Robin Milner, and Mads Tofte. Unifying exceptions with constructors in Standard ML. LFCS Report Series ECS-LFCS-88-55, Laboratory for Foundations of Computer Science, Edinburgh University, Mayfield Rd., EH9 3JZ Edinburgh, U.K., June 1988.

[4] Andrew W. Appel. A critique of Standard ML. *Journal of Functional Programming*, 3(4):391–429, October 1993.

[5] Andrew W. Appel and David B. MacQueen. A Standard ML compiler. In Gilles Kahn, editor, *Functional Programming Languages and Computer Architecture*. ACM, Springer-Verlag, Sept 1987.

[6] Lennart Augustsson and Thomas Johnsson. Lazy ML user's manual. Technical report, Department of Computer Science, Chalmers University of Technology, 1987.

[7] Dave Berry. The Edinburgh SML Library. Technical Report ECS-LFCS-91-148, Laboratory for Foundations of Computer Science, Department of Computer Science, Edinburgh University, April 1991.

[8] Dave Berry. Lessons from the design of a Standard ML library. *Journal of Functional Programming*, 3(4):527–552, October 1993.

[9] Lars Birkedal, Nick Rothwell, Mads Tofte, and David N. Turner. The ML Kit (Version 1). Technical Report DIKU-report 93/14, Department of Computer Science, University of Copenhagen, Universitetsparken 1, DK-2100 Copenhagen, 1993.

[10] R. M. Burstall and R. Popplestone. POP-2 reference manual. In Dale and Michie, editors, *Machine Intelligence 2*. Oliver and Boyd, 1968.

[11] Rod Burstall and Joseph A. Goguen. Putting theories together to make specifications. In *Proc. Fifth Int'l Joint Conf. on Artificial Intelligence*, pages 1045–1058, 1977.

[12] Rod Burstall, David MacQueen, and Donald Sannella. HOPE: An experimental applicative language. In *Proc. 1980 LISP Conference*, pages 136–143, Stanford, California, 1980. Stanford University.

[13] Guy Cousineau, Pierre-Louis Curien, and Michel Mauny. The categorical abstract machine. *Science of Computer Programming*, 8, May 1987.

[14] H. B. Curry. Modified basic functionality in combinatory logic. *Dialectica*, 23:83–92, 1969.

[15] Luis Damas and Robin Milner. Principal type schemes for functional programs. In *Proc. Ninth ACM Symposium on Principles of Programming Languages*, pages 207–212, 1982.

[16] Luis Manuel Martins Damas. *Type Assignment in Programming Languages*. PhD thesis, Edinburgh University, 1985.

[17] Thierry Despeyroux. Executable specifications of static semantics. In Gilles Kahn, David MacQueen, and Gordon Plotkin, editors, *Semantics of Data Types*, volume 173 of *Lecture Notes in Computer Science*. Springer Verlag, June 1984.

[18] E.R. Gansner and J.H. Reppy (eds.). The Standard ML Basis Library reference manual. (In preparation).

[19] Michael Gordon, Robin Milner, and Christopher Wadsworth. *Edinburgh LCF: A Mechanized Logic of Computation*, volume 78 of *Lecture Notes in Computer Science*. Springer Verlag, 1979.

[20] M.J.C. Gordon, R. Milner, L. Morris, M.C. Newey, and C.P. Wadsworth. A metalanguage for interactive proof in LCF. In *Proc. Fifth ACM Symposium on Principles of Programming Languages*, Tucson, AZ, 1978.

[21] Robert Harper and Mark Lillibridge. A type-theoretic approach to higher-order modules with sharing. In *Proc. Twenty-First ACM Symposium on Principles of Programming Languages*, pages 123–137, Portland, OR, January 1994.

[22] Robert Harper and Mark Lillibridge. A type-theoretic approach to higher-order modules with sharing. In *Conference Record of POPL '94: 21st ACM SIGPLAN-SIGACT Symposium on Principles of Programming Languages*, pages 123–137. ACM Press, January 1994.

[23] Robert Harper, David MacQueen, and Robin Milner. Standard ML. Technical Report ECS–LFCS–86–2, Laboratory for Foundations of Computer Science, Edinburgh University, March 1986.

[24] Robert Harper, Robin Milner, and Mads Tofte. A type discipline for program modules. In *Proc. Int'l Joint Conf. on Theory and Practice of Software Development (TAPSOFT)*, pages 308–319. Springer-Verlag, Mar. 1987. Lecture Notes in Computer Science, Vol. 250.

[25] Robert Harper and John C. Mitchell. On the type structure of Standard ML. *ACM Trans. on Prog. Lang. and Sys.*, 15(2):211–252, April 1993.

[26] J. Roger Hindley. The principal type scheme of an object in combinatory logic. *Transactions of the American Mathematical Society*, 146:29–40, 1969.

[27] Stefan Kahrs. Mistakes and ambiguities in the Definition of Standard ML. Technical Report ECS-LFCS-93-257, Dept. of Computer Science, University of Edinburgh, 1993.

[28] Peter J. Landin. The next 700 programming languages. *Comm. ACM*, 9(3):57–164, 1966.

[29] Xavier Leroy. Polymorphism by name. In *Proc. Twentieth ACM Symposium on Principles of Programming Languages*, January 1993.

[30] Xavier Leroy. Manifest types, modules and separate compilation. In *Conference Record of POPL '94: 21st ACM SIGPLAN-SIGACT Symposium on Principles of Programming Languages*, pages 109–122. ACM Press, January 1994.

[31] Xavier Leroy. The Caml Special Light system. Software and documentation available on the Web, `http://pauillac.inria.fr/csl/`, 1995.

[32] D. MacQueen. Modules for Standard ML. In *Conf. Rec. of the 1984 ACM Symp. on LISP and Functional Programming*, pages 198–207, Aug. 1984.

[33] David MacQueen. Using dependent types to express modular structure. In *Proc. Thirteenth ACM Symposium on Principles of Programming Languages*, 1986.

[34] David. B. MacQueen. Structures and parameterisation in a typed functional language. In *Proc. Symposium on Functional Programming and Computer Architecture*, Aspinas, Sweden, 1981.

[35] David B. MacQueen and Mads Tofte. A semantics for higher-order functors. In Donald Sannella, editor, *Proceedings of the 5th European Symposium on Programming (ESOP)*, volume 788 of *Lecture Notes in Computer Science*, pages 409–423. Springer-Verlag, 1994.

[36] John McCarthy. *LISP 1.5 Programmer's Manual*. MIT Press, 1956.

[37] D. Meredith. In memoriam Carew Arthur Meredith. *Notre Dame Journal of Formal Logic*, 18:513–516, 1977.

[38] Robin Milner. A theory of type polymorphism in programming languages. *J. Computer and Systems Sciences*, 17:348–375, 1978.

[39] Robin Milner. How ML evolved. *Polymorphism: The ML/LCF/Hope Newsletter*, 1(1), 1983.

[40] Robin Milner. Changes to the Standard ML core language. Technical Report ECS-LFCS-87-33, Laboratory for Foundations of Computer Science, Edinburgh University, 1987.

[41] Robin Milner and Mads Tofte. *Commentary on Standard ML*. MIT Press, 1991.

[42] Robin Milner, Mads Tofte, and Robert Harper. *The Definition of Standard ML*. MIT Press, 1990.

[43] James H. Morris. *Lambda Calculus Models of Programming Languages*. PhD thesis, MIT, 1968.

[44] Colin Myers, Chris Clack, and Ellen Poon. *Programming with Standard ML*. Prentice Hall, 1993.

[45] Lawrence C. Paulson. *ML for the Working Programmer (2nd edition)*. Cambridge University Press, 1996.

[46] Lawrence C. Paulson. *Logic and Computation: Interactive Proof with LCF*. Cambridge Tracts in Theoretical Computer Science. Cambridge University Press, 1987.

[47] Gordon Plotkin. A structural approach to operational semantics. Technical Report DAIMI–FN–19, Computer Science Department, Aarhus University, 1981.

[48] John A. Robinson. A machine-oriented logic based on the resolution principle. *J. ACM*, 12(1):23–41, 1965.

[49] Donald Sannella and Andrzej Tarlecki. Program specification and development in Standard ML. In *Proc. Twelfth ACM Symposium on Principles of Programming Languages*, New Orleans, 1985.

[50] Ryan Stansifer. *ML Primer*. Prentice Hall, 1992.

[51] Chris Stone and Robert Harper. A type-theoretic account of Standard ML 1996. Technical Report CMU-CS-96-136, School of Computer Science, Carnegie Mellon University, School of Computer Science, Carnegie Mellon University, Pittsburgh, PA 15213-3891, May 1996.

[52] David Tarditi, Greg Morrisett, Perry Cheng, Chris Stone, Robert Harper, and Peter Lee. TIL: A type-directed optimizing compiler for ML. In *Proc. ACM SIGPLAN Symposium on Programming Language Design and Implementation*, Philadelphia, PA, May 1996.

[53] Mads Tofte. *Operational Semantics and Polymorphic Type Inference*. PhD thesis, Edinburgh University, Department of Computer Science, Edinburgh University, Mayfield Rd., EH9 3JZ Edinburgh, May 1988. Available as Technical Report CST-52-88.

[54] Mads Tofte. Type inference for polymorphic references. *Information and Computation*, 89(1), November 1990.

[55] Mads Tofte. Principal signatures for higher-order program modules. *Journal of Functional Programming*, 4(3):285–335, July 1994.

[56] Jeffrey D. Ullman. *Elements of ML Programming*. Prentice Hall, 1994.

[57] Andrew Wright. Simple imperative polymorphism. *Journal of Lisp and Symbolic Computation*, 8(4):343–355, December 1995.

# Index

Concepts that are associated with a special name (e.g, a meta-variable or a mathematical symbol) are listed under both the special name and the full name, often with the former entry being a *see* reference to the latter. For example, "value binding" is indexed as follows:

Items are ordered lexicographically, by extending the usual alphabetical ordering on letters using the rule *space = hyphen < symbol or greek letter < digit < latin letter*. Upper and lower case letters are regarded as equal and font does not affect ordering.

Adjective-noun compounds are normally found under the noun. For example, "non-expansive expression" is found under "expression".

The index includes concepts and identifiers which were present in the 1990 Definition but are absent in SML '97.

## W

## Y